NOW
IS THE ACCEPTABLE TIME

A TIME FOR EVERY MATTER UNDER HEAVEN

TOM KINGERY

Copyright © 2023 Tom Kingery.

All rights reserved. No part of this book may be reproduced, stored, or transmitted by any means—whether auditory, graphic, mechanical, or electronic—without written permission of both publisher and author, except in the case of brief excerpts used in critical articles and reviews. Unauthorized reproduction of any part of this work is illegal and is punishable by law.

All Scriptures are from the New Revised Standard Version unless otherwise noted.

ISBN: 979-8-88640-708-2 (sc)
ISBN: 979-8-88640-709-9 (hc)
ISBN: 979-8-88640-468-5 (e)

Because of the dynamic nature of the Internet, any web addresses or links contained in this book may have changed since publication and may no longer be valid. The views expressed in this work are solely those of the author and do not necessarily reflect the views of the publisher, and the publisher hereby disclaims any responsibility for them.

One Galleria Blvd., Suite 1900, Metairie, LA 70001
1-888-421-2397

CONTENTS

Introduction 1

Chapter 1   A Time to Be Born, and a Time to Die 7

Chapter 2   A Time to Plant, and A Time to Pluck Up 15

Chapter 3   A Time To Kill, And A Time to Heal 22

Chapter 4   A Time to Break Down, And a Time to Build Up 30

Chapter 5   A Time to Weep and a Time to Laugh 37

Chapter 6   A Time to Mourn, and a Time to Dance 43

Chapter 7   A Time to Embrace, and a Time to Refrain
            from Embracing 54

Chapter 8   A Time to Seek, and a Time to Lose 60

Chapter 9   A Time to Keep, and a Time to Throw Away 66

Chapter 10 A Time to Tear, and a Time to Sew 71

Chapter 11 A Time to Keep Silence, and a Time to Speak 77

Chapter 12 A Time to Love, and a Time to Hate 85

Chapter 13 A Time for War, and a Time for Peace 92

Conclusion: Now is the day of salvation 99

INTRODUCTION

> As we work together with him,
> we urge you also not to accept the grace of God in vain.
> For he says,
> "At an acceptable time I have listened to you,
> and on a day of salvation I have helped you."
> See, now is the acceptable time,
> now is the day of salvation
> 2 Corinthians 6:2

What does "now" mean to you? Is it "this moment"? Is it "the present"? What could "now" mean from the perspective of eternity? In eternity there is no passing of time. In eternity "a day is like a thousand years and a thousand years are like a single day" (2 Peter 3:8). "A thousand years in your sight are like yesterday when it is past, or like a watch in the night" (Psalm 90:4)

Does the apostle Paul imply that time is running out? Is an opportunity about to pass? Is there a risk in missing something? That can't be true, can it? After all, Paul wrote these verses over 19 centuries ago! And I believe the final "now" has not yet come. But I also believe that "Now *is* the acceptable time!"

There is a "now" in everyone's life that comes where there is a moment of decision. That "now" fulfills our purpose in eternity, and it brings focus to God's design for our lives. It can be the moment when we discover: "That's what it's all about!" It could be the moment we hear and respond to our calling. However that "now" manifests itself to us, it can bring a sense of direction, or completion, or, change, or, at a minimum, inspiration.

Some theologians might call it a "God-moment". But it seems to be an encounter with something greater than ourselves, something beyond our minds. It can be a moment of recognition as well as definition. It shows us to ourselves and it defines us to some degree. It may give us a sense of our place in God's Plan, or God's Kingdom. Either way, we are renewed by such moments. They can give us a sense of rebirth, of awareness, or of a new consciousness. In fact there can be many "nows" in our lives.

The writer of Ecclesiastes realized that such "nows" occur in many ways, and said, "There is a time for every matter under heaven" (Ecclesiastes 3:1b). These "nows" will be the substance of this book. In Ecclesiastes, the writer has given 14 opposing pairs, set as dichotomies of issues human beings might face. They will be the subjects of each chapter.

1. A time to be born, and a time to die
2. A time to plant, and a time to pluck up what is planted
3. A time to kill, and a time to heal
4. A time to break down, and a time to build up
5. A time to weep, and a time to laugh
6. A time to mourn, and a time to dance
7. A time to throw away stones, and a time to gather stones together
8. A time to embrace, and a time to refrain from embracing
9. A time to seek, and a time to lose
10. A time to keep, and a time to throw away
11. A time to tear, and a time to sew
12. A time to keep silence, and a time to speak
13. A time to love, and a time to hate
14. A time for war, and a time for peace

Realize, before we begin, that I do not see a legitimate progression from one pair to the next. They sometimes feel arbitrarily listed, but they round out the human experience fairly well. There could easily be more such dichotomies, like a time to stay, and a time to go; or, a time to fear, and a time to trust; or a time for business, and a time for play… but I don't feel a need to add to what this passage of scripture gives us.

And realize that there is an acceptable time for every matter under heaven. However "now" presents itself, we can meet it with the grace of faith, and we can greet it with the hope of wisdom. The message I want to share includes seeing each of these "nows" through the lens of *my* faith, and, interpreting them in the light of Christian belief. Seize the moment.

SCRIPTURES

To discover more about what the Bible says about time, here are some scripture passages that will help to inspire us:

> Esther 4:14 – "For if you keep silence at such a time as this, relief and deliverance will rise for the Jews from another quarter, but now, you and your family will perish. Who knows? Perhaps you have come to royal dignity for just such a time as this."
>
> Ecclesiastes 3:11 NIV – He has made everything beautiful in its time. He has also set eternity in the human heart; yet no one can fathom what God has done from beginning to end."
>
> Galatians 4:4 – But when the fullnes of time had come, God sent his Son…
>
> Ephesians 1:8b-10 – With all wisdom and insight he has made known to us the mystery of his will, according to his good pleasure that he set forth in Christ, as a plan for the fullness of time, to gather up all things in him, things in heaven and things on earth.
>
> Ephesians 5:15-16 – Be careful then how you live, not as unwise people but as wise, making the most of the time, because the days are evil.
>
> Colossians 4:5 – Conduct yourselves wisely toward outsiders, making the most of the time.

WHAT TO DO

Think about how you have experienced God-moments in your life. What happened?

> Consider the question, What does "now" mean to you?
>
> Think about what opportunities may have come your way. Are you letting them pass you by? Or do you take advantage of them?
>
> Think about the ways you may be here for "such a time as this."
>
> Think about what it might mean to "make the most of the time."
>
> Don't think of time as a flowing stream, but as the arrival of a "now."

A PRAYER

Almighty God, You have given us this moment in time, help us seize the day. Help us rise to the occasion. Help us to find Your purpose working in our hearts. And help us to decide to live by Your will for our journeys. May we hear Your calling and discover Your Plan every day. This we ask in Jesus's name. Amen.

A POEM

A Time Has Come

A time has come upon the earth
For souls to waken, for rebirth,
For all alive to be aware
Of a power so great, so good, so rare,
That neglecting it would not be wise.
This is our shot, and hope is the prize.

Let's all dream of a wonderful day
When everyone will find a way
To touch the bliss by which we're blessed,
Till every heart becomes possessed
By glory, triumph, majesty;
And our beliefs will set us free.

Let us fan the flames of this desire
For the time has come to feed this fire.

CHAPTER 1

A TIME TO BE BORN, AND A TIME TO DIE

> We do not live to ourselves, and we do not die to ourselves.
> If we live, we live to the Lord, and if we die, we die to the Lord;
> so then, whether we live or whether we die,
> we are the Lord's.
> Romans 14:7-8

Everything has a lifespan. It seems only natural to begin by discussing "a time to be born, and a time to die." In Psalm 31, we are given these words of truth: "I trust in you, O Lord; I say, 'You are my God.' My times are in your hand." The whole Psalm is a prayer for deliverance from some enemy or enemies, but we can see the writer entrusting himself into God's keeping. He knows "My times are in your hand."

We all need to say this. Paul says it: "Whether we live or whether we die, we are the Lord's" (Romans 14:8). The Psalmist even went so far as to say, "You knit me together in my mother's womb" (Psalm 139:13b). In verse 16 of that Psalm, he says, "Your eyes beheld my unformed substance. In your book were written all the days that were formed for me, when none of them as yet existed." Does this imply that God knows everything about us before we were even born, or, is the writer saying this about the way he feels about his own existence? I tend to lean toward the latter, simply because we have free will, and can make choices that effect our destiny.

But what if our story is already in place before it begins. It seems worth exploring, but, not now.

For now, let's focus on birth and death.

A Time to Be Born

Have you ever wished you had been born in a different time? I have known some people who wished they had lived in another era in a different land. I think they are, for the most part, imagining a better lifestyle of some kind. They fantasize about the special beauty of, for example, France in the early 1770s, and the glory of being a noble courtier. But… what if they were born a pauper? What if the worst part of that era was their lot? The point to be made is that we don't get to choose when we are born.

But we are here, now. We can't change that fact… yet. I dont believe there will ever be such a thing as time-travel (mostly because, so far as we know :), no one has returned to our time from the future!); but like Mordecai told Esther, "Who knows? Perhaps you have come to royal dignity for just such a time as this" (Esther 4:14b). The story suggests that we can have a sense of destiny concerning the times in which we live. Perhaps the example of the clarion call coming from many environmentalists is being expressed for "such a time as this!"

We can often sense a purpose in our lives that inspires us to seize the day, to act as if what we might do might make a difference. God may have a plan for our lives, but still, we have to cooperate with that plan. We can cooperate, or we can resist. What I believe we need to do is be intentional. We need to adopt Paul's vision for our lives:

> "We know that all things work together for good for those who love God, who are called according to his purpose. For those whom he foreknew he also predestined to be conformed to the image of his Son, in order that he might be the firstborn within a large family. And those whom he predestined he also called; and those whom he called he also justified; and those whom he justified he also glorified (Romans 8:28-30).

Again, the foreknowledge idea can be an expression of a very personal sense of destiny, and Paul is making it universal. If it is meant to be universal, for everyone, I have some questions: About whom does God *not* have foreknowledge? Who is not called or predestined or justified?

Many scholars qualify things by emphasizing the phrase "those who love God." Their idea is that it is *only* those who love God who get to experience all things working together for good. Only "those who love God" are called, foreknown, and predestined. But again, if God knew ahead of time that someone would love Him, did they have a choice? And, if God knew ahead of time that someone would not love him, couldn't God, as powerful as He is, have altered that? If not, why did He come as Jesus Christ to save the lost? (See Luke 19:10 – "For the Son of Man came to seek and to save the lost."). Ultimately, we must choose to love God, or, not.

Being Born

There is a "time to be born." When we come into this world it is our time. Moreso, in a big way, it is our mother's time. God had been "knitting us together within our mothers' wombs," and *her* time came to give us birth. Thank you, mom! It may all happen within God's timing, so we also need to thank God. But we are given life. With the cooperation of our mothers, God gives us all as gifts to the world (and to our parents as well… and to our families, our friends, our social networks, etc.).

Each of us have a date of birth. It was recorded and put on a "Birth Certificate." I don't know what it actually certifies, other than the date and time and place of our delivery; but it seems to become relevant at different stages of our lives, and, as I have learned, even at our time of death, which seems a little weird. But we come into this world totally dependent. We need to realize that without others we would never have lived till now. Our births set in motion so many cycles of care that we should be glad to be alive today. But God didn't bring us this far just to bring us this far!

We're here. And we need to accept the fact.

But we are also able to be "born again!" There is a time to be born again. Many people acknowledge a certain day for their born-again experience. In the Gospel of John Jesus told Nicodemus, "No one can see the kingdom of God with out being born from above." (3:3) The words "from above" can also be translated "anew." Jesus reiterates this in verse 5 where He says, "No one can enter the kingdom of God without being born of water and the Spirit."

For most followers of Christ, this re-birth is another "now" moment. More than a realization, it is truly a fulfillment, an inspiration. An awareness arrives and in many respects we are given new life. We are often given a sense of having a part in God's Plan. It is all a gift of God's grace. And we begin to live in the light of God's grace. And, we begin to see the truth of what Paul said in Romans 14: "We do not live to ourselves, and we do not die to ourselves. If we live, we live to the Lord, and if we die, we die to the Lord; so then, whether we live or whether we die, we are the Lord's" (14:7-8)

By our birth and by our re-birth we belong to God, "We are the Lord's." God claims us as His own. And we affirm it in our belief. As we do, though, we also learn that it is time for our old selves to die!

A Time To Die

We all die. Everything has a lifespan. From the point of view of the world, we all hope to leave a legacy; we hope there will be some reason to be remembered. Even if it's only that we lived for awhile, the world will know we were here. And hopefully the world will be better for knowing that. One thing we should all hope for is that we will have done something that made the world a better place.... for someone if not for everyone.

As Christians, from the point of view of faith, we learn that dying is not just an end. Because we believe in the Resurrection, we believe in eternal life, which may begin now, but begins to be fulfilled when we die. So dying is not just dying. Meanwhile, as I said, our old selves need to die off. Paul said, "Put away your former way of life, your old self, corrupt and deluded by its lusts, and be renewed in the spirit of your minds, and so clothe yourselves with the new self, created according to the likeness of God in true righteousness and holiness" (Ephesians 4:22-24). Paul also said, "I have been crucified with Christ, and it is no longer I who live, but it is Christ who lives in me... (Galatians 2:19b-20). Jesus said, "If anyone would come after me, let him deny himself and take up his cross daily and follow me" (Luke 9:23).

There is something that not only needs to be denied, it needs to pass away. There is a time to die. It begins when we are reborn! And it may take the rest of our lives to completely die in this way. But <u>now</u> is the acceptable time!

So there is the cycle of life and death, renewal and relinquishing, coming and going. Let us find the blessings in it all. Let us be a blessing through it all.

SCRIPTURES

To discover more about what the Bible says about dying to self, here are some scripture passages that will help to inspire us:

> Matthew 7:13-14 – Enter through the narrow gate; for the gate is wide and the road is easy that leads to destruction, and there are many who take it. For the gate is narrow and the road is hard that leads to life, and there are few who find it.

> Luke 14:27 – Whoever does not carry the cross and follow me cannot be my disciple.

> John 11:25-26 – "I am the resurrection and the life. Those who believe in me, even though they die, will live, and everyone who lives and believes in me will never die."

> Romans 6:1-2 – What then shall we say? Should we continue in sin in order that grace may abound? By no means! How can we who died to sin go on living in it?

> Romans 6:8 – But if we have died with Christ, we believe that we will also live with him.

> Romans 8:38-39 – For I am convinced that neither death, nor life, nor angels, nor rulers, nor things present, nor things to come, nor powers, nor height, nor depth, not anything

else in all creation, will be able to separate us from the love of God in Jesus Christ our Lord.

1 Corinthians 15:21-22 – Since death came through a human being, the resurrection of the dead has also come through a human being; for as all die in Adam, so will all be made alive in Christ.

2 Corinthians 5:17 – So if anyone is in Christ, there is a new creation; everything old has passed away; see, everything has become new!

Galatians 5:24-35 – Those who belong to Christ Jesus have crucified the flesh with its passions and desires. If we live by the Spirit, let us also be guided by the Spirit.

Philippians 1:21 – For to me, living is Christ and dying is gain.

Colossians 3:10 – Do not lie to one another, seeing that you have stripped off the old self with its practices and have clothed yourselves with the new self, which is being renewed in knowledge according to the image of its creator.

1 Peter 2:24 – He himself bore our sins in his body on the cross, so that, free from sins, we might live for righteousness; by his wounds you have been healed.

WHAT TO DO

Reckon yourself dead to sin and alive to God. (Romans 6:11)

Think about, if you could choose when and where you were born, when would that be? Why?

Think about how you feel about being born in *this* time.

Consider destiny. What is it? What is yours?

Ask yourself, What is my purpose?

Think: What do you think about "predestination"?

Think about "free will." How free are we?

Ask yourself, what does it mean that "God didn't bring us this far just to bring us this far."

If you have been "born anew", recount how it happened. What does it mean?

Ask yourself, "What will be my legacy?"

Ask yourself, "What does it mean to 'die to self?'" Are you "crucified with Christ"? Have you "died to sin"?

A PRAYER

Almighty God, author of life, give us the grace to accept the lives you have given us, and the courage to face the end of life. Help us to learn to live in Your light and walk by Your Spirit; and help us to know that by dying we will rise to life eternal. Just give us the grace we need to make the most of the time we have been given. This we ask in Jesus's name. Amen.

A POEM

When The Days for Me to Die Arrive

When the days for me to die arrive,
I pray that I will have been truly alive.
I pray that my life will have been all complete,
And the song of my soul will still be this sweet.
I only ask that once I am gone,
Something about my faith will live on.
I want all to know that it wasn't about me,
'Cause it's all about Jesus and what life can be
When we follow His teaching, His will, and His Way;
And we walk in the light of His glorious Day.

I pray that my death will be life in my Lord,
And my soul will be blessed and delivered restored.
I pray that the beauty I know in life now
Will have even more splendor than this mind can allow.

CHAPTER 2

A TIME TO PLANT, AND A TIME TO PLUCK UP

>He told them many things in parables, saying,
>"Listen!
>A sower went out to sow.
>And as he sowed, some seeds fell on the path,
>and the birds came and ate them up.
>Other seeds fell on rocky ground, where they did not have much soil,
>and they sprang up quickly, since they had no depth of soil.
>But when the sun rose, they were scorched,
>and since they had no root, they withered away.
>Other seeds fell among thorns,
>and the thorns grew up and choked them.
>Other seeds fell on good soil
>and brought forth grain,
>some a hundredfold, some sixty, some thirty.
>Let anyone with ears listen."
>Matthew 13:3-9

When God created Adam, he was placed in the Garden of Eden. His purpose was to till it and keep it (Genesis 1:15). This is the earliest purpose for humankind. Every time I planted a vegetable garden, I felt like, to some degree, I identified with the purpose of Adam. But there was so much tilling to do after the seeds I planted began to grow. Weeds grew too. I imagine there would have been no weeds in Paradise, of course. The tilling there was just to keep the Garden from growing too much. So, I was sort of jealous of Adam. Weeds didn't begin to grow until after the Fall. Then the ground outside of Eden was cursed (Genesis 3:17), and thorns and thistles would grow (Genesis 3:18). So the hard work of gardening with which I became so familiar, was in all the weeding. Necessary to prevent the seeds from being "choked" by the "thorns" as in the Parable of the Sower.

What impresses me the most about gardening is the miracle of growth. From a single seed, planted in good soil, roots emerge and shoots sprout, sunshine, water, and nutrients from the soil give them growth, and, in time, the plants produce their fruits (vegetables). Sometimes, as with carrots, for example, the root *is* the fruit! And if you need to improve the soil, what do you add to it? Fertilizer. Fertilizer is often made from manure. Sometimes, you just shovel manure right on to the soil where you're going to plant. Imagine that! Something kind of gross can help a garden! Egyptians learned early-on that dead fish buried beneath the seeds did a good job of aiding the growth. And, likewise, clippings from the lawn, leaves, and even weeds could be piled together purposefully to mulch into compost, which could turn into soil, and be used to bring nutrients to the garden. It is all part of the wonderful miracle of growth, producing food, and keeping a garden

Planting and Plucking

There is often a definite time to plant. It is in the springtime, after winter. And the time for planting has a very "now" feeling to it. If you plant too early, a late cold spell could ruin your plans. If you plant too late, an early autumn frost could spoil the vegetables. So there is also a fairly narrow window for harvesting. When the word "pluck" is used in this dichotomy, I tend to think of grapes, or olives, fruit trees, or figs, or even nuts. When it's a vegetable garden, it becomes more of a time for picking. Either way, it is a matter of gathering in. Some plants produce over a long enough period that you can pick the vegetables when you notice they are ripe enough; like tomatoes or zuchinis. But it is a wonderful gift to receive these fruits of our labors.

Of course, a reason to pluck up what is planted, is after the in-gathering is done, the plants no longer need to be absorbing nutrients from their soil. Plucking them, and then allowing the stems, roots, and leaves to deteriorate is a way of letting this garden "waste" return nutrients back to the soil.

Now, when Jesus explains the Parable of the Sower, He explains that the seeds are "the word of the kingdom" (Matthew 13:18). There is always a time to plant kingdom seeds. People can hear about the kingdom any time. But the harvest is more of a matter of bearing fruit (13:23), as in good works and righteousness. In the Sermon on the Mount, Jesus says, "You will know them by their fruits" (Matthew 7:16, 20). He is talking about false prophets, and He says, "Every good tree bears good fruit, but the bad tree bears bad fruit. A good tree cannot bear bad fruit, nor can a bad tree bear good fruit. Every tree that does not bear good fruit is cut down and thrown into the fire" (Mathew 7:17-19). That's pretty harsh sounding. I better do my best to produce good fruit! Right?

A few chapters later, at the end of Matthew's Chapter 9, Jesus says, "The harvest is plentiful but the laborers are few; therefore ask the Lord of the harvest to send out laborers into his harvest" (vs 37-38). It's curious that he says this after describing the crowds that followed Him as being like sheep without a shepherd (Matthew 9:36). There is no doubt, though, that He wants to gather these lambs into The Fold; meanwhile, every lamb, or, follower is like a field of planted seeds. It's also curious that He speaks about seeds and sowing while He is at the beech (13:2). I have wondered why he didn't talk about catching fish there. He does later, though.

Harvest time is coming! We need to think of the in-gethering of souls. God wants to draw us in to His Kingdom, where Jesus is our King. We need to see ourselves as good soil for the kingdom-seeds. Then we will "hear the word and understand it" (Matthew 13:23)? Take advantage of this time. The harvest is here! "Now is the time!"

SCRIPTURES

To discover more about what the Bible says about a harvest, here are some scripture passages that will help to inspire us:

Genesis 8:22 – As long as the earth endures, seedtime and harvest. Cold and heat, summer and winter, day and night, shall not cease.

Exodus 23:16 – You shall observe the festival of harvest, of the first fruits of your labor, of what you sow in the field. You shall observe the festival of ingathering at the end of the year, when you gather in from the fields the fruit of your labor.

Leviticus 26:3-5 – If you follow my statutes and keep my commandments and observe them faithfully, I will give you your rains in their seasons, and the land shall yield their fruit. Your threshing shall overtake the vintage, and the vintage shall overtake the sowing; you shall eat your bread to the full and live securely in your land.

Psalm 126:5-6 – May those who sow in tears reap with shouts of joy. Those who go out weeping, bearing the seed for sowing, shall come home with shouts of joy, carrying their sheaves.

Isaiah 9:3 – You have multiplied the nation, you have increased its joy; they rejoice before you as with joy at the harvest, as people exult when dividing the plunder.

Jeremiah 51:33 – For thus says the Lord of hosts, the God of Israel: Daughter Babylon is like a threshing floor at the time when it is trodden; yet a little while, and the time for her threshing will come.

Matthew 13:30 – Let both of them grow together until the harvest; and at harvest time I will tell the reapers, 'Collect the weeds first and bind them in bundles to be burned, but gather the wheat into my barn.'"

2 Corinthians 9:6 – The one who sows sparingly will also reap sparingly, and the one who sows bountifully will also reap bountifully.

2 Corinthians 9:10 – He who supplies seed to the sower and bread for food will supply and multiply your seed for sowing and increase the harvest of your righteousness.

Galatians 6:7-9 – Do not be deceived; God is not mocked, for you reap whatever you sow. If you sow to your own flesh, you will reap corruption from the flesh; but if you sow to the Spirit, you will reap eternal life from the Spirit. So let us not grow weary in doing what is right, for we will reap at harvest time, if we do not give up.

Hebrews 12:11 – Now, discipline always seems painful rather than pleasant at the time, but later it yields the peaceful fruit of righteousness to those who have been trained by it.

Revelation 14:15-20 – Another angel came out of the temple, calling with a loud voice to the one who sat on the cloud, "Use your sickle and reap, for the hour to reap has come, because the harvest of the earth is fully ripe. So the one who sat on the cloud swung his sickle over the earth, and the earth was reaped. Then another angel came out of the temple in heaven, and he too had a sharp sickle. Then another angel came out from the altar, the angel who has authority over fire, and he called with a loud voice to him who had the sharp sickle, "Use your sharp sickle and gather the clusters of the vine, for its grapes are ripe." So the angel swung his sickle over the earth and gathered the vintage of the earth, and he threw it into the great wine press of the wrath of God. And the wine press was trodden outside the city, and blood flowed from the wine press as high as a horse's bridle, for a distance of about two hundred stadia.

WHAT TO DO

Plant a garden. Participate in the miracle of growth.

Start a compost pile. Let nothing go to waste.

Keep farmers in your prayers. They depend a lot on good weather, good soil, and growth.

Think about the soils in the parable of the sower. How has your life been like the path? How has it been like rocky ground? ….like the thorns? …. Like the good soil?

Be sure you see the word of the kingdom as the seeds that are sown. Where do you get these seeds?

Think about how your life has produced good fruit.

Become a "laborer for the harvest".

Read the Parable of the Weeds and the Wheat. Take it as a warning for those who are not producing fruit.

Sow bountifully.

A PRAYER

Almighty God, You have given us the purpose of tilling and keeping the garden that is this earth. Give us grace to care for the soil and to sow bountifully; to work for growth and participate in the glorious harvest You will bring. Especially, Lord, give us the wisdom and the faith we need to be a part of the harvest of righteousness that is surely coming. This I ask in Jesus's name. Amen.

A POEM

Simple Seeds of Peace

In the garden of our souls
      Let's plant simple seeds of peace,
Where everything that sprouts and grows
      Will always flourish and increase.
We will somehow know the pleasure
      Of a happy, grateful heart,
And we'll gladly store up treasure
      That will set us all apart.
Let's also scatter love abroad
      So we can harvest joy.
Even angels will, with thrill, applaud
      The perfect vision we deploy.

      May every garden bring the sight
      Of heaven's hope and total light.

CHAPTER 3

A TIME TO KILL, AND A TIME TO HEAL

*Jesus went throughout Galilee, teaching in their synagogues
and proclaiming the good news of the kingdom of God
and curing every disease and every sickness among the people.
So his fame spread throughout all Syria,
and they brought to him all the sick,
those who were afflicted with various diseases and pains,
demoniacs, epileptics, and paralytics,
and he cured them.
Matthew 4:23-24*

Euthanasia became a very popular issue about 40 years ago. I can't comply with euthanasia for human beings. I believe too strongly in what Paul says in Romans 14:7-8 m from Chapter 1, which says, "We do not live to ourselves, and we do not die to ourselves. If we live, we live to the Lord, and if we die, we die to the Lord; so then, whether we live or whether we die, we are the Lord's." Our lives belong to God. But so do our deaths. I also do not believe in prolonging someone's existence just because we can. I know that death, from the point of view of the medical field, is generally seen as a failure. Something they could have done should have worked. But, from the point of view of faith, death is not an enemy. I do not think it is wrong to let "nature" take its course, though. Like I said, death is not an enemy. Death is a natural part of existence.

A Time to Kill

Still, there is a time to kill. I believe what the Hebrew people did when they sacrificed animals for offerings, for reconciliation, and for their sacred rituals in the tabernacle – that was the "time to kill." Yes, the Hebrew Law pronounced judgment on some grievous sins, but it was, as often as not, a way of "purging the evil from their midst" (Deuteronomy 17:7). I don't like the death penalty. I think it is a matter of trying to "play God" with someone's life. I believe in what Paul said above in Romans 14:7-8 – *our lives and our deaths belong to God.*

Even war was prescribed or ordered in the Old Testament. But, I believe war is always wrong. Going to war meant that some form of diplomacy had failed. The idea of conquest is sinful, and often reflects a meglomaniacal ego seeking some self-importance. I can accept the ideal of self defense, though, as long as it doesn't become overly retributive. Jesus' instructed his followers to "turn the other cheek" (Matthew 5:38-40). We are not supposed to resist an evil person. Now I don't think Jesus was promoting the idea of passive resignation. He wants us to be peacemakers (Matthew 5:9). We need to do all we can to promote "getting along." But still, we would be foolish to place ourselves or others in danger. We are not supposed to just let ourselves be abused.

I don't really want to spend more time than necessary to defend my point of view about death, killing, war, or capital punishment. My main idea is that in the Hebrew sacrificial system, there was a prescribed time for killing… animals. Somehow the sins of persons were to be seen as being transmitted into the animal, and then killing the animal somehow brought atonement. Even with Christians, it was acknowledged that "without the shedding of blood there is no forgiveness of sins" (Hebrews 9:22). But it is the blood of Christ that makes "atonement" for the sins of the world. "Once for all" (Hebrews 10:10).

I eat meat, and I rarely give it a second thought that an animal had to be killed so I could do so. But, if we didn't want to eat meat, there is nothing wrong with that, as far as I am concerned. Often, the remains of the animals butchered can be used in fertilizers. So, there is a full cycle in the life and death of those animals.

That there is a time to kill is not a matter of killing for killing's sake. We are intentional about it. If it supports life we tend to condone it. But only then, as food. I have heard many stories about pets who have had to be "put down." It is merciful to do so. Animals don't understand the redeeming nature of suffering the way humans can. Maybe, if there has been an infestation of some kind, we would not hesitate to do away with some critters. But we don't make animal sacrifices any more. Not since the destruction of the Temple in Jerusalm in 70 AD.

A Time to Heal

What is important about this dichotomy is that there *is* a time to heal. And healing can happen all the time. There is no time that is not a time to heal. Every scar I have is proof that, though I was injured or wounded, God was working in me by His grace healing me as well. And, I'm sure, God has healed you as well. Even a scratch or a blister that is no longer seen is a sign of the power of God within us to heal. Our bodies, as frail as they sometimes are, are also very resilient. The ways our bodies work to bring healing are abundant and amazing. We can go through some extremely trying times, whether it is surgery to remove a malignancy, or, an operation to mend a bone. We can return, sometimes, stronger than before. I think the only thing that does not heal is old age, and I'm feeling that more and more every year. I am definitely not what I used to be.

Sometimes, we need to take time to heal. It's called recovery. And recovery takes more time than we usually think. Often, within the process of recovery, there is rehabilitation. But there is also rest. And rest is restoration. Our bodies can be restored. After we've been sick, after we have mended, there is some down-time. We do less and just take time. If we don't give ourselves the time we need, if we feel good enough to be "active", often we over do it, and we need to give ourselves more rest the next day. I know that has been the way it is with me. And I've witnessed it in many others. We get ambitious. Sometimes though, the more we do, within reason, the more we *can* do. Bit by bit, we can be restored.

This was not the case with my wife. She had MS (Multiple Sclerosis), which, we learned, back in 1988, in time will usually progress. The weakness did not dissipate, and she finally lost the use of her legs, and spent the last two years of her life in bed. She became my calling. I did more for her as time went on. In some ways, it brought out the best in me. I was a caregiver, a comforter, a helper. Sometimes just rolling Carol over made a huge difference in her comfort. But there were times when she was too weak to feed herself, and I would sit beside her and spoon her food to her mouth.

Healing in her circumstance was more emotional than physical. She immersed herself more deeply in her faith, trusting God for every next hour. And I was inspired. Her perfect healing came on May 13th, 2019. Her final triumph! It was her time to die. But…only her body died.

But there is a time for *healing*. All throughout the New Testament we can see the healing ministry of Christ. Even at the beginning of His ministry, "Jesus went throughout Galilee, teaching in their synagogues and proclaiming the good news of the kingdom of God and curing every disease and every sickness among the people" (Matthew 4:23). During His existence and with the presence of His Spirit after He ascended it has been a time to heal! We can rejoice in this time. We are truly blessed.

Some of the healing stories in the Gospels give us a powerful message. Bartimaeus was a blind man in Jericho. His hearing told him that a large crowd was passing by. Someone told him it was Jesus. He called out. Jesus finally had them bring Bartimaeus forward. "Then Jesus said to him, 'What do you want me to do for you?' The blind man said to him, 'My teacher, let me see again.' Jesus said to him, 'Go, your faith has made you well.' Immediately he regained his sight and followed him on the way" (Mark 10:51-52). An interesting point is made here. Bartimaeus cried out for mercy. Mercy comes in many forms, but for him it would be sight. But he had to be particular. "Let me see again."

Often, Jesus needs to know what we want. It was his trust in Jesus, his faith, that made Bartimaeus well.

There is a time to heal. And it is *all the time*. We need to be particular, though. We want the climate to heal. We want the brokenness between nations to heal. Do we ask for these things? We want divisions to mend; we want alienation to alleviate. Do we ask for these things? Our faith can make us well. We need to ask for faith to manifest itself wherever healing is needed. Faith can truly make a difference.

SCRIPTURES

To discover more about what the Bible says about healing, here are some scripture passages that will help to inspire us:

> Exodus 15:26 – If you will listen carefully to the voice of the Lord your God, and do what is right in his sight, and give heed to his commandments and keep his statutes, I will not bring upon you any of the diseases that I brought upon the Egyptians; for I am the Lord who heals you.
>
> Deuteronomy 32:39 – See now that I, even I, am he; there is no god besides me. I kill and I make alive; I wound and I heal; and no one can deliver from my hand.
>
> Psalm 6:2 – Be gracious to me, O Lord, for I am languishing; O Lord, heal me, for my bones are shaking with terror.
>
> Psalm 30:2 – O Lord, my God, I cried to you for help, and you have healed me.
>
> Psalm 103:1-5 – Bless the Lord, O my soul, and all that is within me, bless his holy name. Bless the Lord, O my soul, and and do not forget all his benefits – who forgives all your iniquities, and heals all your diseases, who redeeems your life from the Pit, who crowns you with steadfast love and mercy, who satisfies you with good as long as you live so that your youth is renewed like the eagle's.
>
> Psalm 147:3 – He heals the brokenhearted, and binds up their wounds.
>
> Isaiah 41:10 – Do not fear, for I am with you, do not be afraid, for I am your God; I will strengthen you, I will help you, I will uphold you with my victorious right hand.

Isaiah 53:4-5 – Surely he has borne our infirmities and carried our diseases; yet we accounted him stricken, struck down by God and afflicted. But he was wounded for our transgressions, crushed for our iniquities; upon him was the punishment that made us whole, and by his bruises we are healed.

Isaiah 57:18-19 – I have seen their ways, but I will heal them; I will lead them and repay them with comfort. Creating for their mourners the fruit of the lips. Peace, peace, to the far and the near, says the Lord; and I will heal them.

Jeremiah 33:6 – I am going to bring it recovery and healing; I will heal them and reveal to them abundance of prosperity and security.

Matthew 8:16-17 – That evening they brought to him many who were possessed with demons; and he cast out the spirits with a word, and cured all who were sick. This was to fulfill what had been spoken through the prophet Isaiah, "He took our infirmities and bore our diseases."

Philippians 4:19 – My God will fully satisfy every need of yours according to his riches in glory in Christ Jesus.

James 5:14-15 – Are any among you sick? They should call for the elders of the church and have them pray over them, anointing them with oil in the name of the Lord. The prayer of faith will save the sick, and the Lord will raise them up; and anyone who has committed sins will be forgiven.

1 Peter 2:24 – He himself bore our sins in his body on the cross, so that, free from sins, we might live for righteousness; by his wounds you have been healed.

WHAT TO DO

Pray for healing. Pray in particular ways.

Let restoration happen. Give it time.

Think about how you feel with respect to killing animals for food.

Think about how you feel with respect to physician-assisted suicide.

Think about how you feel about "letting nature take its course."

Think of how our bodies seem to heal, sometimes, without our even doing anything.

Be confident in God's healing power. Trust it.

A PRAYER

Almighty God, You have healed me, and even now, You are healing me. Restore my health; deliver me from my sickness and my wounds. I only ask for Your will to be done in my body. I do believe that it is a time to heal. So I also ask for You to give me words that heal and comfort and care. Give us all such compassion that we may walk with the Lamb of God and become apart of what can take away the sins of the world. This I ask in Jesus's name. Amen.

A POEM

I Am Broken

I am broken. I need mending.
It's a cycle never ending.
Sometimes I just want sympathy.
Sometimes I want to be set free.
Sometimes I want my pain to ease.
I want the simple luxuries
Of peace and love and happiness.
Take my anguish, leave me blessed.
Take my torment and my sorrow.
Make me strong just for tomorrow.
Give me healing, Lord, I pray.
Help me make it through this day.
      And when I'm well and I can smile,
      Help me stay that way awhile.

CHAPTER 4

A TIME TO BREAK DOWN, AND A TIME TO BUILD UP

"What sign can you show for doing this?"
Jesus answered them,
"Destroy this temple, and in three days I will raise it up."
The Jews then said,
"This temple has been under construction for forty-six years,
and you will build it up is three days?"
But he was speaking of the temple of his body.
After he was raised from the dead,
his disciples remembered that he had said this.
John 2:18-22a

Nothing really lasts forever. Everything seems to need rebuilding eventually. Especially in areas where hurricanes, tornadoes, floods, fires, or earthquakes have happened, sometimes in the course of a single lifetime, we know there will be several times of rebuilding. Curiously, though, there are ancient ruins all over the world. Some are shrouded in mystery and we don't know exactly why those locations were abandoned. Others were destroyed in some cataclysmic event, like an earthquake or a volcano or a war. Archeology is a fascinating subject for me. Many sites in ancient Israel show more than one layer (strata) of building and rebuilding. Sometimes it is known what had happened to the old structures, and who rebuilt the site. But imagine people from our distant future examining the ruins where we once lived. What might they find and what could they tell about the ways we lived our lives? That is part of what archeologists do. Very interesting.

The reality, though is that there come times of breaking down and building up. What needs to break down in your life? What needs to be built up?

A Time to Break Down

A classical image of "breaking down" comes from Isaiah 5:4-7 where there is a love song about a vineyard –

> "What more was there to do for my vineyard that I have not done to it? When I expected it to yield grapes, why did it yield wild grapes? And now I will tell you what I will do to my vineyard. I will remove its hedge, and it shall be devoured; I will break down its wall, and it shall be trampled down. I will make it a waste; it shall not be pruned or hoed, and it shall be overgrown with briers and thorns; I will also command the clouds that they rain no rain upon it. For the vineyard of the Lord of hosts is the house of Israel…"

It is a parable of sorts. The prophet declares seven woes on the people of Israel, for their sinful ways. And God will no longer protect His "vineyard." Sin is a breakdown. It is a straying, and it is a falling away from our purpose in God and Christ; it is a failure to live up to our covenant of obedience, and it is like going in the wrong direction.

Without detailing the breakdown of the people of Israel, the reality was that God would be relinquishing them to the conquest of their enemies. Their cities would be left in ruins, the walls protecting them would be destroyed, and God's care, though still present, would not deliver them from their enemies. Such a time to break down was meant to humble the people enough to arouse repentance for their wrongs, to encourage hope. To inspire them to walk in God's ways and live within God's covenant.

The good news was that a time would come for the faithful to return and rebuild. In a previous book (*We Rejoice in Our Suffering*), I likened spiritual growth to the images of building a house. The first thing that is done is some tearing down, and digging up, in order to lay a solid foundation. This is what breaking down needs to mean for us. We break down *in order* to build up. Often, in ancient times, building materials from a tear-down were used in new construction. Sometimes, today. In fact, the United Methodist parsonage in Galena was built with materials used to bear ammunition and cannons to the Savanna Army Depot several miles south of Galena. The wood of the crates was still perfectly fine to be reused. It just seems unusual for some reason.

War can be a horrible break down. Spiritually speaking, "we do not wage war according to human standards; for the weapons of our warfare are not merely human, but they have divine power to destroy strongholds. We destroy arguments and every proud obstacle raised up against the knowledge of God, and we take every thought captive to obey Christ" (2 Corinthians 10:4-5). The battles we are supposed to wage are spiritual and moral battles. The end is reconstructing our relationships with God, by building one another up.

A Time to Build Up

So the very important task is always to build up. Rebuilding is spoken about many times in prophetic proclamations. Isaiah foresaw the rebuilding of ancient ruins (Isaiah 58:12; 61:4). Nehemiah tells the story of the return of the faithful and the rebuilding of the temple. I am always impressed that home builders can take open space and create a house there. I am also impressed that an old building can be torn down and something modern can be constructed in its place. I have volunteered for Habitat for Humanity on several homes. I feel a sense of pride for having had a small part in helping to create a home for someone else.

Whatever we may build can leave a trace of who we are. During our lives, it is always a time to build. Yes, there will need to be a process of tearing down, sometimes. But, we're not just supposed to tear things down. Peter tells us to be "living stones," to "let yourselves be built into a spiritual house" (1 Peter 2:5)

Jesus told His naysayers who wanted some kind of sign for his authority to cleanse the Temple and cast out the moneychangers, that the sign would be: "'Destroy this temple, and in three days I will raise it up.' The Jews then said, 'This temple has been under construction for forty-six years, and you will build it up in three days?' But he was speaking of the temple of his body" (John 2:19-21). The Resurrection is the epitome of rebuilding. And in Christ we are raised. We receive new life by His grace and love. We are rebuilt.

How wonderful it is to build someone up. I can remember Junior High friends doing their best to one-up each other on putting someone down. I guess they thought their insults were funny. Even the one kid being put down laughed at what they were saying. But I felt insulted for the guy. How much easier it would be to bring light and acceptance into someone's life. "Therefore encourage one another and build each other up, as indeed you are doing" (1 Thessalonians 5:11). It is always a time for this kind of building.

SCRIPTURES

To discover more about what the Bible says about building and rebuilding, here are some scripture passages that will help to inspire us:

> Nehemiah 4:6 – So we rebuilt the wall, and all the wall was joined together to half its height; for the people had a mind to work.
>
> Psalm 127:1 – Unless the Lord builds the house, those who build it labor in vain.
>
> Proverbs 24:3 – By vision a house is built, and by understanding it is established.
>
> Isaiah 58:12 – Your ancient ruins shall be rebuilt; you shall raise up the foundations of many generations; you shall be called the repairer of the breach, the restorer of streets to live in.

Isaiah 61:4 – They shall build up the ancient ruins, they shall raise up the former devastations; they shall repair the ruined cities, the devastations of many generations.

Jeremiah 1:10 – "See, today I appoint over nations and over kingdoms, to pluck up and to pull down, to destroy and to overthrow, to build and to plant."

Jeremiah 31:4 – Again I will build you, and you shall be built, O virgin Israel! Again you shall take your tambourines, and go forth in the dance of the merrymakers.

Micah 7:11 – A day for the building of your walls! In that day the boundary shall be extended.

Acts 15:16-17 – "After this I will return, and I will rebuild the dwelling of David, which has fallen; from its ruins, I will rebuild it, and I will set it up, so that all other peoples may seek the Lord – even all the Gentiles over whom my name has been called…"

2 Corinthians 5:1 – For we know that if the earthly tent we live in is destroyed, we have a building from God, a house not made with hands, eternal in the heavens.

1 Peter 2:4-8 – Come to him, a living stone, though rejected by mortals yet chosen and precious in God's sight, and like living stones, let yourselves be built into a spiritual house, to be a royal priesthood, to offer spiritual sacrifices to God through Jesus Christ. For it stands in Scripture: "See, I am laying in Zion a stone, a cornerstone chosen and precious; and whoever believes in him will not be put to shame." To you then who believe, he is precious; but for those who do not believe, "The stone that the builders rejected has become the very head of the corner," and "A stone that makes them stumble, and a rock that makes them fall." They stumble because they disobey the word, as they were destined to do.

WHAT TO DO

Watch a documentary on some of the ancient ruins being excavated by archeologists today. What happened to turn them into ruins? What is learned about the people who lived there?

Watch a video about a building's destruction. With dynamite in all the right places, a tall building can be brought down in seconds. It's amazing. Of course, realize that the purpose of its destruction may have been some breakdown or flaws in its construction, or, at least, to make way for some new construction.

Think: How is spiritual growth like building a house?

Think about how war is a sign of some sad breakdowns. What should have been done?

Study the stories of Israel's conquest. Learn about the destruction that was wrought. And, likewise, learn about the reconstruction.

Think about what you would like to see built in the world today. What are we building for the generations yet to come?

Think about ways you can build others up in faith.

A PRAYER

Almighty God, You encourage us with the vision of our own resurrection. By faith we will be made new. It is like being rebuilt, so we give thanks for this hope. Give us grace to encourage one another and to build each other up. Let us be like living stones. Build us together into a spiritual house. Tear down what is faulty in our lives, and rebuild us with Your love, in Your purpose, for the glory of Your Kingdom. In Jesus's name we pray. Amen.

A POEM

Don't Tear Down the Old

Don't tear down the old just to build something new.
The past still has lessons for me and for you.
Count every blessing, they're all very real.
We don't always need to invent a new wheel.

If we could begin with what we might find
When we scrutinized things that once were designed
To offer the best and the fullest of dreams,
We'll find the old flow in today's hopeful streams.

But when we discover the foundation has cracks,
It calls for a time when everyone acts;
And we all come together to work and rebuild.
Discovering our purpose and how it's fulfilled.

The plans of today aren't to tear down the past,
But to build a new future with visions more vast.

CHAPTER 5

A TIME TO WEEP AND A TIME TO LAUGH

Rejoice with those who rejoice, weep with those who weep.
Romans 12:15

The right time to weep or laugh is oftened determined by what others are doing. I think Paul is right in Romans 12:15 – "Rejoice with those who rejoice, weep with those who weep." You might not feel that way at that moment, but you have a reason. Of course, when we are personally sad, it's all right to weep; and when we are personally happy, it's all right to laugh. Be true to yourself. Don't be pretentious. But, when Paul spoke of the working of the Church, the Body, he said, "If one member suffers, all suffer together with it; if one member is honored, all rejoice together with it" (1 Corinthians 12:26).

Created in God's likeness, we know God experiences emotions. So it is not wrong to be emotional. A problem comes, however, when we overdo it. We can let anger or resentment stew within us until it bubbles up and we go too far. It can turn to hate. Haman did that with respect to Mordecai. He didn't like Mordecai, and he let hatred grow in his heart. Then, because Mordecai was a Jew, he began to hate all Jews. The story is the framework for the book of Esther. Please, note that there are no scriptures that encourage people to hate with those who hate; or to be angry with those who are angry, etc. Politicians sometimes find reasons to blame their opposition as part of some problem based on issues they might favor. During the Civil Rights movement of the 1960s, many campaigned against their opposition based solely on what they considered to be ideas that were either too liberal or too conservative for the changing times. It was like some thought it was wrong to weep for those who cried out for justice. And, it was like some thought it was wrong to rejoice in the triumphs of traditional values many thought not to change.

Sometimes it takes a good measure of discernment to sort out what to do. But God wants us to hear the cries of the afflicted, to understand the groaning of the suffering, and to be compassionate for the sake of those in misery. God also wants us to celebrate the joys and triumphs of those who have reasons to rejoice.

A Time to Weep

We are not supposed to harden our hearts concerning the feelings and the needs of others. Jesus pronounces a blessing over those who mourn: "they will be comforted" (Matthew 5:4). In the Gospel of Luke, Jesus said, "Blessed are those who weep now, for you will laugh" (Luke 6:21b). We need to hear the cries of those who weep. They should not be ignored. When we hear them, our hearts are tweaked into action. We want to do something that will alleviate their grief. And, we grieve with them and for them.

Sympathy can be a wonderful motivator. After a hurricane devastates a neighborhood, leaving homes, streets, and businesses deluged by floods, I can't help but want to do something. It doesn't make sense for me, at my age, to go there to help, but there are always needs for the resources that can help people recover. Those resources cost money, and there are missions in place that can meet the needs. So the natural thing for me to do is send some financial support to enable those service organizations. It may sound like I'm just throwing money at the cause, but I know for a fact that those on the front lines working for the recovery appreciate every ounce of assistance they get. I may weep with those who weep, but they work with those who are devastated, and I am glad they are there.

I simply want to do unto others what I wish others would do for me if I was in their place (Matthew 7:12).

Our greatest reason to weep is the awareness of sin, oppression, and falsehood; and how so many people that could know Christ, or, know

Him better, don't. The darkness in this world needs our light! ...as much as our sympathy.

A Time to Laugh

If you have ever known someone with a contagious laugh, you just love to join their presence. Laughter is good medicine. Actually, the Proverb says that "a *cheerful heart* is good medicine" (Proverbs 17:22). But the sign of a cheerful heart is often smiles and laughter. It is hard not to laugh when people around you are laughing. Sometimes joy is catching. And that may be part of why we like comedies and comediens.

When I was in France (1977) at an outdoor cafe with some American friends, we were joking and laughing and just having a good time. A Frenchman sitting nearby acknowledged our spirit and he said it was nice to see our cheerfulness. I told him that this was what life was all about. But I don't think I convinced him. And I realized, after some conversation, that Americans are generally perceived by much of the world as extremely light-hearted, not often serious. But again, there is a time for every purpose under heaven. At the time, our purpose was enjoyment. We were in France, after all! The time to be serious would surely come, and it keeps coming. Still, let's keep a light-heartedness about us. Enjoy the world that God has given us.

When we can't rejoice with those who rejoice, something is wrong. It's like the couple in the restaurant that just got engaged, and everybody applauds, even though the others may not know them. They are still glad for them. At least we should be. The soldier returning home to surprize his wife and children is welcomed with so much joy that it brings everyone to tears. It may be a time to rejoice, but it is just so touching that it stirs our hearts and tweaks our emotions. So we wipe our eyes with a smile on our face!

Our greatest reason for joy is Jesus Christ. He may not make me laugh, but I rejoice to know what He has done for me, and, for you.

SCRIPTURES

To discover more about what the Bible says about laughter and weeping, here are some scripture passages that will help to inspire us:

1 Samuel 30:3-4 – When David and his men came to the city, they found it burned down, and their wives and sons and daughters taken captive. Then David and the people who were with him raised their voices and and wept, until they had no more strength to weep.

Job 8:21 – He will yet fill your mouth with laughter, and your lips with shouts of joy.

Job 30:25 – Did I not weep for those whose day was hard? Was not my soul grieved for the poor?

Psalm 30:11 – You have turned my mourning into dancing; you have taken off my sackcloth and clothed me with joy.

Psalm 42:5 – Why are you cast down, O my soul, and why are you disquieted within me? Hope in God; for I shall again praise him, my help and my God.

Psalm 96:11-12 – Let all the heavens be glad, and let the earth rejoice; let the sea roar, and all that fills it; let the field exult, and everything in it. Then shall all the trees of the forest sing for joy before the Lord…

Proverbs 17:22 – A cheerful heart is good medicine, but a downcast spirit dries up the bones.

Ecclesiastes 8:15 – I commend enjoyment, for there is nothing better for people under the sun than to eat, and drink, and enjoy themselves, for this will go with them in their toil through the days of life that God gives them under the sun.

Isaiah 55:12 – For you shall go out in joy, and be led forth in peace; the mountains and the hills before you shall burst into song, and all the trees of the field shall clap their hands.

Jeremiah 9:1 – O that my head were a spring of water, and my eyes a fountain of tears, so that I might weep day and night for the slain of my poor people!

Luke 2:10 – But the angel said to them. "Do not be afraid; for see – I am bringing you good news of great joy for all people…

Luke 6:25b – "Woe to you who are laughing now, for you will mourn and weep."

John 15:11 – I have said these things to you so that my joy may be in you, and that your joy may be complete.

1 Peter 1:8 – Although you have not seen him, you love him; and even though you do not see him now, you believe in him and rejoice with an indescribable and glorious joy…

WHAT TO DO

Think about letting others give the cue about whether to weep or to laugh. Is that always right?

Do it: "Rejoice with those who rejoice, weep with those who weep" (Romans 12:15).

Think about how you have over-reacted emotionally. What were the circumstances? How did you get carried away?

Think ahead of time about how you will sort out what to do.

Think: For what do you weep? For what do you rejoice?

Ask yourself: How has sympathy motivared you?

Let your joy become contagious!

A PRAYER

Almighty God, You have given us our greatest reason to rejoice by giving us Your Son; but we have many reasons to weep because we are such sinners. I would rather rejoice than weep, but I can do both when needed. Give me grace to focus on my reasons to rejoice, but help me hear the cries of the afflicted, for I will then do all I can to alleviate their suffering. Please, help me be what You want me to be whenever I can. I ask this prayer in Jesus's name. Amen.

A Poem

Let's Do Our Best to Laugh

Let's do our best to laugh today
    Someone needs to hear it.
It may not be from words we say,
    But they will catch the spirit.
We know another time will come
    When joy will be the past.
But let's delight in where we're from
    And then let's make it last.
We come from knowing heaven's taste,
    From the triumph of belief,
Before some doubt snuck in to waste
    And steal it like a thief.
        Today, though, let's be very glad
        That we can have what we have had.

CHAPTER 6

A TIME TO MOURN, AND A TIME TO DANCE

> For the Lord has ransomed Jacob,
> and has redeemed him from hands too strong for him.
> They shall come and sing aloud on the height of Zion,
> and they shall be radiant over the goodness of the Lord,
> over the grain, the wine, and the oil, and over
> the young of the flock and the herd;
> their life shall become like a watered garden,
> and they shall never languish again.
> Then shall the young women rejoice in the dance,
> and the young men and the old shall be merry.
> I will turn their mourning into joy,
> I will comfort them, and give them gladness for sorrow.
> Jeremiah 31:11-13

Grief has a process. There are natural times for grief and mourning: Someone has died, or, something was lost. We may not really *want* to grieve, but, there *is* a time to weep, and it often involves a time to mourn. The scriptures validate times of mourning, but they rarely leave it there. "Weeping may linger for the night, but joy comes in the morning" (Psalm 30:5b). Often the cause for mourning is not planned. Many losses come rather unexpectedly.

Mourning is directly related to weeping. Whereas weeping is emotional, mourning makes it formal. Weeping includes internal grief over suffering and loss, while mourning is often ritualized and very ourwardly intentional. Weeping may be personal, while mourning can be corporate. People can rally behind the causes for weeping, but they definitely come together to mourn. Often, when someone dies, friends of the survivors come to comfort them and one another. Sometimes, people gather to celebrate the blessings of the life that was lost, especially if it was a good, long life. Funerals can be wonderful times of reunion and celebration; but they can also be wonderful times of care and support. All can be relevant, and all can be helpful.

A Time to Mourn

The grief process has no time limit. Though some cultures may suggest there should or could be. Acceptance of a loved one's loss can be difficult. Grieving can last much longer than we would wish. One woman told me, as the first Thanksgiving and Christmas since her husband died were approaching, that she didn't want to ruin the holidays for everyone because all she could do, all the time, was cry. She wanted to be strong for her family. We prayed together about this, and afterwards it came to me to let her know that "tears are not a sign of weakness, but of grief." She should feel no shame for her sadness. In fact, her sadness could give permission to the rest of her family ro weep with the one who weeps.

Denial can be a part of the grief process. "They can't be gone! I can still feel their presence!" People can also deny the pain of their grief. "It's not that big a deal. Life goes on." Though that may be true to some degree, the grieving process still needs time. There may be other "stages" of grief, but mourning can bring healing. Eventually, by grace, the time for mourning can give way to renewed joy, and even, a time to dance.

A Time to Dance

When my wife, Carol, died in 2019, I decided, and I claimed that "There was more reason to rejoice in her triumph than for me to grieve my loss." When someone in Christ dies, we believe they have entered into eternal life; and that can be a very positive thing. We need to do a better job of claiming this truth. Truly, joy comes with the new day, *as* a new day. And soon enough there will come a time to celebrate, to rejoice, and even, to dance!

I think dancing is a celebration of life. We move to the music in fun and funny ways. It reveals the light-heartedness the world often needs. While mourning may be a time to take things seriously, dancing is a time to take things lightly. From the point of view of faith, I believe we should see all of life is a time of light. Remember, "even the darkness is not dark to you; the night is as bright as the day, for darkness is as light to you" (Psalm 139:12).

Even though our hearts may be broken, we can still dance!

SCRIPTURES

To discover more about what the Bible says about mourning and dancing, here are some scripture passages that will help to inspire us:

> Matthew 5:4 – Blessed are those who mourn, for they will be comforted.
>
> Psalm 34:18 – The Lord is near to the brokenhearted, and saves the crushed in spirit.
>
> Psalm 73:26 – My flesh and my heart may fail, but God is the strength of my heart and my portion forever.
>
> Psalm 147:3 – He heals the brokenhearted, and binds up their wounds.
>
> Psalm 150:4 – Praise him with tambourine and dance…
>
> Isaiah 41:10 – Do not fear for I am with you, do not be afraid, for I am your God; I will strengthen you, I will help you, I will uphold you with my victorious right hand.
>
> Matthew 11:16-17 – "To what shall I compare this generation? It is like children sitting in the marketplaces and calling out

to one another, 'We played the flute for you, and you did not dance; we wailed, and you did not mourn.'"

John 14:27 – Peace I leave with you; my peace I give to you. I do not give as the world gives. Do not let your hearts be troubled, and do not let them be afraid.

John 16:22 – So you have pain now; but I will see you again, and your hearts will rejoice, and no one will take your joy from you.

Romans 8:18 – I consider that the sufferings of this present time are not worth comparing with the glory about to be revealed to us.

WHAT TO DO

Compare God's glory to "the sufferings of this present time." Does it turn your mourning into dancing?

Remember why you have danced in the past. What was the reason?

Think about those for whom you have mourned. Remember them joyfully now.

Think about why you have grieved. Who was it for? Do you still grieve?

Think about how mourning can include healing. How?

Review the relationship between mourning and weeping; as well as the relationship between rejoicing/laughing and dancing.

Consider the ways you like to celebrate life.

A PRAYER

Almighty God, Lord of our time, help us to hear the music of the world, and let it move us in Life's Dance. When we have witnessed tragedies and days of darkness, years of pain, give us glimmers of Your light that we may see what gives us hope. And in the aftermath of grief, let us comfort every heart that has been broken or weighed down. Help us all to see the truth that guides us and the love of Christ that draws us forward. This I pray in Jesus's name. Amen.

A SONG

Remember How You Used to Dance

Remember how you used to dance night after night,
Song after song, faster and faster? You did all right!
Life was so fun. Joy was so easy. You seemed to free!
Never forget how wild and how crazy your heart used to be!
    It seems like only yesterday.
    Or is it really far away?

It makes me want to dance again,
    To hear the songs that moved us all.
Our lives were just so full back then.
    Or was it that the hours were small
        And easier to fill and simpler in style?
        Or maybe it was just easier to smile?

    You liked to dance. It was just you.
    Or was there nothing else to do?

A Time to Throw Away Stones, and a Time to Gather Stones Together

> Come to him, a living stone,
> though rejected by mortals
> yet chosen and precious in God's sight,
> And like living stones,
> let yourselves be built into a spiritual house,
> to be a holy priesthood,
> to offer spiritual sacrifices acceptable to God through Jesus Christ.
> For it stands in scripture:
> "See, I am laying in Zion a stone, a cornerstone
> chosen and precious;
> and whoever believes in him will not be put to shame."
> 1 Peter 2:4-6

Two purposes, and, a third: First, clear the farmland of stones. Second, gather those stones as building materials. And third, be like stones, living stones.

It only makes sense to clear our land of the stones big enough to be in the way of the plow. They are impediments and obstacles. And, then, gather those stones together to build roads and walls, and houses; and even monuments.

A Time to Throw Away Stones

First I want to encourage everyone wanting to stone sinners to throw away your stones. Jesus told the self-righteous people so ready to condemn an adulteress, "Let anyone among you who is without sin be the first to throw a stone at her" (8:7). No one is righteous enough to condemn another to death. We cannot play God… though we should uphold the law. We are all accountable to God. It can feel powerful to be able to condemn what is evil; but… "No one is righteous, not even one" (Romans 3:10). It is a time to throw away those stones!

Because stones were a primary building material back in Biblical times, it is probably more true that the process of clearing fields and roads of large stones was also a time when they were gathered for future developments. Stones were rarely just "cast away." But like stumbling blocks, they needed to be removed. I'll wager that there was a practical division of labor between those who cleared the fields and those who gathered the stones to a building site.

But think about what might need to be removed from the fertile soil of your life. We can always go to the Parable of the Sower (Matthew 13:3-9; Mark 4:3-9 and Luke 8:5-8), partly because it's about the hindrances to hearing the word of the kingdom, and that's what stones in a field can be – hindrances.

Hindrances and obstacles can come in many forms. There can actually be objects that are in the way. They can make forward progress difficult or slow. If you've ever gone hiking, you know what I mean; though I *do* like to see stepping stones in a creek. Some things, and even people can be in the way. We don't just throw them away, but we can usually choose who to include in our journeys. Many wise people recommend the purging of toxic people from our lives. For me, the more important issue is the toxic thoughts that hinder our understanding and our spiritual growth. Wrong thoughts lead to sinful behavior. And that's not good. "Whatever is true, whatever is honorable, whatever is just, whatever is pure, whatever is pleasing, whatever is commendable, if there is any excellence and if there is anything worthy of praise, think about these things" (Philippians 4:8)

A Time to Gather Stones Together

We all need the appropriate building blocks of life. If we do not use them correctly, our foundation may be faulty, our walls may crumble, and our roads may be bumpier than we want them to be. Several times in scripture there were directives to gather stones to make a memorial monument. With no images allowed, sometimes they simply set the stones into an interesting pattern, or, just a pile. It was an intentional process to establish a memory.

I knew a man from Scotland, he showed us his slides one night. Scotland is beautiful. I loved the stone walls that seemed everywhere, surrounding fields and homes, and along the lanes and roads. I'm sure there are many places in the world that look very similar. But my memories of my Scottish friend's slides stand out. Walls like that are built from the stones in the soil. There must have been a lot of stones in Scotland, because there are a lot of walls!

Stones *can* be used as weapons. Remember Goliath? I like the quote that says, "While everyone was afraid of Goliath because he was too big to hit, David simply said he was too big to miss!" (Don't know where it comes from). Einstein said that "I know not with what weapons WWIII will be fought, but **WWIV will be fought with sticks and stones**."

Precious gems are a special kind of stone. If you are fortunate to gather some of them together, count yourself specially blessed. The high priest at the temple wore a special breastplate that had 12 precious stones in it, representing the 12 tribes of Israel.

Christians are called by Peter to become living stones with Christ. How do we do that? Well, not by being hard and unmoveable. We need to see ourselves, together, as part of the new temple for the Kingdom of Christ. Christ is the "cornerstone" (1 Peter 2:6), "chosen and precious" (1 Peter 2:3). "To you who believe, he is precious; but for those who do not believe, 'The stone that the builders rejected has become the head of the corner,' and 'A stone that makes them stumble, and a rock that makes them fall.' They stumble because they disobey the word…" (1 Peter 2:7-8).

Be a stone!

This dichotomy might seem to be a natural one to connect with the 4th about breaking down and building up. It seems like it should precede the 4th dichotomy. I see it as separate simply because the purposes are so different. And, I see them as connected simply because stones were the most common building material in biblical times. The biggest difference is that there is no actual breaking down in this one. Though there is a casting off, it seems a lot less destructive. And though there seems to be no actual building suggested, it implies, for me, the accumulation of building materials. Build!

SCRIPTURES

To discover more about what the Bible says about stones, here are some scripture passages that will help to inspire us:

> Genesis 31:45-46 – So Jacob took a stone, and set it up as a pillar. And Jacob said to his kinfolk, "Gather stones," and they took stones and made them a heap and they ate there by the heap.
>
> Joshua 4:6b-7 – When your children ask in time to come, "What do these stones mean to you?" then you shall tell them that the waters of the Jordan were cut off in front of the ark of the covenant of the Lord. When it crossed over the Jordan, the waters of the Jordan were cut off. So these stones shall be to the Israelites a memorial forever.
>
> 1 Kings 5:17-18 – At the king's command, they quarried out great, costly stones in order to lay the foundation of the house with dressed stones. So Solomon's builders and Hiram's builders and the Gebalites did the stonecutting and prepared the timber and the stone to build the house..
>
> 2 Chronicles 14:6-7 – He built fortified cities in Judah while the land had rest. He had no war in those years, for the Lord gave him peace. He said to Judah, "Let us build these cities, and surround them with walls and towers, gates and bars; the land is still ours because we have sought the Lord our God; we have sought him, and he has given us peace on every side." So they built and prospered.
>
> Isaiah 62:10 – Go through, go through the gates, prepare the way for the people; build up, build up the highway, clear it of stones, lift up an ensign over the peoples.
>
> John 8:7 – "Let anyone among you who is without sin be the first to throw a stone at her."

WHAT TO DO

Cast away the hindrances in your life. Clear the soil.

Think about the stones you may need to throw away. Why are you holding on to them?

Think: Are there any toxic people in your life? Why? What makes them toxic?

Think: What are some toxic thoughts? Superiority? Prejudice? Indifference? Relaxed moral expectations? Why might these be toxic?

A PRAYER

Almighty God, You are present in the hearts of believers; so whatever is not welcome by Your Spirit in me, help me remove. Give me grace to let go of what is toxic and wrong. And help me gather for You what You want me to have. This I ask in Jesus's name. Amen.

A POEM

Stumbling Blocks and Paving Stones

Let's all bring our stumbling blocks
Together to make paving stones.

And then let's build a great wide way
that truly leads us somewhere new,
where everyone will want to go.

And then let's build a monument
To all the trips-and-falls-and-rise-agains.

And then let's build a castle fortress
Where we can feel safe inside
And catch our breath and find some rest
And talk about what we've been through.

Not to brag or prove ourselves
But just to give each other time
And just to give each other space

Forgetting there were stumbling blocks.

CHAPTER 8

A TIME TO EMBRACE, AND A TIME TO REFRAIN FROM EMBRACING

She (Wisdom) is a tree of life to those who lay hold of her;
those who hold her fast are called happy.
Proverbs 3:18

Embrace the truth. Refrain from lies. Embrace faith. Refrain from sin. Embrace goodness. Refrain from evil.

Often, when we think of embracing, we think of an affectionate action. That's not wrong, but it is not all "embracing" can mean. Of course, we should always embrace others with the love in our hearts. And we should especially hold fast to our husbands, wives, children, and parents. Scripture expresses "embracing" in many ways. It involves "holding fast," either to loved ones, or, to ideas. It includes "keeping", as in keeping the commandments, and keeping vows. To embrace certain ideas is to adhere or hold fast to them.

I have already spoken about how we need to cast away the stones that are hindrances in our lives. But we also need to refrain from embracing them. What we need to embrace is the truth, the love, the goodness of faith.

A Time to Embrace

It is natural to want to embrace those you love. But some settings are inappropriate for many displays of affection. That's when we need to refrain from being too emotional in our expressions. A handshake is a form of embrace, though. Most of the time, it is just a way of greeting each other. I like hugs, but not every time. Some people are a bit too "huggy" for me.

Christians believe in "holding fast to what is good" (Romans 12:9). In Romans 12, Paul exhorts believers to discover many behaviors that we need to embrace. We need to see these as more than just ideas; they are a prescription for righteous living.

> Let love be genuine; hate what is evil, hold fast to what is good; love one another with mutual affection; outdo one another in showing honor. Do not lag in zeal, be ardent in spirit, serve the Lord. Rejoice in hope, be patient in suffering, persevere in prayer. Contribute to the needs of the saints; extend hospitality to strangers.
>
> Bless those who persecute you; bless and do not curse them. Rejoice with those who rejoice, weep with those who weep. Live in harmony with one another; do not be haughty, but associate with the lowly; do not claim to be wiser than you are. Do not repay anyone evil for evil, but take thought for what is noble in the sight of all. If it is possible, so far as it depends on you, live peaceably with all.
>
> Beloved, never avenge yourselves, but leave room for the wrath of God; for it is written, "Vengeance is mine, I will repay, says the Lord." No, "if your enemies are hungry feed them; if they are thirsty, give them something to drink; for by doing this you will heap burning coals on their heads."
>
> Do not be overcome by evil, but overcome evil with good. (Romans 12:9-21)

Embrace these behaviors. Embrace your beliefs. We might accept the truth intellectually, but truly embracing it becomes a heart matter. The time to hold fast to our beliefs is when they are challenged by the ways of the world. James exhorts believers "to keep oneself unstained by the world" (James 1:27). Easier said than done, though. It is hard to be *in* the world but not *of* the world. That's where we need to know what to embrace, and what to refrain from embracing.

Refrain From Embracing

Don't hold on to what is counterproductive in your life. Let go of ideas that do not profit your spiritual growth and development. Be wise. The author of the Proverbs said of wisdom, "She is a tree of life to those who lay hold of her; those who hold her fast are called happy" (Proverbs 3:18). By embracing wisdom, we will develop a natural aversion to folly. And that includes the folly of some ideas. Listen to Paul's advice in his Letter to the Ephesians:

> "Putting away falsehood, let us all speak the truth to our neighbors, for we are members of one another. Be angry, but do not sin, do not let the sun go down on your anger; and do not make room for the devil. Thieves must give up stealing; rather let them labor and work honestly with their own hands, so as to have something to share with the needy. Let no evil talk come out of your mouths, but only what is useful for building up, as there is need, so that your words may give grace to those who hear. And do not grieve the Holy Spirit of God, with which you were marked with a seal for the day of redemption. Put away from you all bitterness and wrath and anger and wrangling and slander, together with all malice, and be kind to one another, tenderhearted, forgiving one another, as God in Christ has forgiven you" (Ephesians 4:25-32).

That is one example of how we need to refrain from embracing wrong and sinful ways. The list goes on in Ephesians 5, and, there are other lists of behaviors to embrace and from which to refrain. But we need to learn what to embrace, and, what avoid. Once we learn these things, we'll know it is a time to embrace, *and*, a time to refrain from embracing.

SCRIPTURES

To discover more about what the Bible says about embracing, here are some scripture passages that will help to inspire us:

Psalm 85:10 – Steadfast love and faithfulness will meet; righteousness and peace will kiss each other.

Proverbs 4:4 – Let your heart hold fast my words; keep my commandments and live.

Philippians 3:12 – Not that I have already obtained this or have already reached the goal; but I press on to make it my own, because Christ Jesus has made me his own.

Philippians 3:16 – Only let us hold fast to hat we have attained.

Acts 4:32 – Now the whole group of those who believed were of one heart and soul, and no one claimed private ownership of any possessions, but everything they owned was held in common.

James 1:27 – Religion that is pure and undefiled before God the Father, is this: to care for orphans and widows in their distress, and to keep oneself unstained by the world.

James 3:2 – All of us make many mistakes. Anyone who makes no mistakes in speaking is perfect, able to keep the whole body in check with a bridle.

1 John 5:21 – Little children, keep yourselves from idols.

Psalm 119:133 – Keep my steps steady according to your promise, and never let iniquity have dominion over me.

WHAT TO DO

Read Romans 12:9-21 again. Here there are many behaviors we need to embrace, the first of which is to love!

Consider wisdom. What is it? What is folly?

Embrace your beliefs. Remember the creeds. Study them. Learn what Jesus wants you to know.

Don't hold on to what is counterproductive in your life.

Think: What does Paul mean by "putting away" certain behaviors in Ephesians 4? What do you need to "put away"?

A PRAYER

Almighty God, You want us to embrace Your ways, You want us to keep Your commandments, and You want us to hold fast to what is good. Help me surrender the bitter resentments I have held on to; give me strength to let go of my wrong and distorted ways of thinking; and give me grace to avoid those things in my path that can be stumbling blocks. I want to embrace Your Kingdom, Your Word, and the Life to which You have called us all. This I pray in Jesus's name. Amen.

A SONG

Let go. I'll catch you. You will not fall.
It will all come together after all.
God wants to bless you. And God is enough.
You just don't need all that other stuff.

The pain and grief you feel won't last.
It's good to leave it all back in the past.
You'll never forget it all the way.
Let it visit, but don't let it stay.

> Let your future be your guide.
> And let your triumphs give you pride.

Embrace the promises you know;
And trust the visions hope can show.
And when the past returns to taunt you,
Don't let the demons try to haunt you.

CHAPTER 9

A TIME TO SEEK, AND A TIME TO LOSE

> Ask, and it will be given you;
> search, and you will find;
> knock, and the door will be opened for you.
> For everyone who asks receives,
> and everyone who searches finds,
> for for everyone who knocks, the door will be opened.
> Matthew 7:7-8

I think of the many who have lost "everything" in a natural disaster who have been wise to say, "We still have our lives." Often, we take for granted all the things we had until they are lost to us. Even the people we might lose along the way. How many old girlfriends told me that they didn't know what they had until after they had broken up with me! I seem to remember dozens! (Haha). For most of them, they usually felt there would be someone better! So losing me was just shedding unwanted baggage.

Though we should never see others as "baggage", sometimes it makes sense to leave some people behind as we go forward. We need to see everyone as temporary gifts that God has given to us. It may seem sad to lose a friend, but life can have such twists and turns; and we may go our separate ways. What can happen is that we will find new friends, new gifts, new paths.

A Time to Seek

I wasn't always seeking the friends I made, but I eventually came to believe that God must have put them in my path for a reason. Often, it is when we are seeking the Lord, that we find someone, or, something new in our lives. But God wants people to seek Him, to seek His Kingdom and His righteousness. God wants us to find the truth, not just so we can say that we know the truth, but so we can apply it to our lives. God even "rewards those who seek him" (Hebrews 11:6).

Faith is a process of seeking even more than it is a well-spring of understanding. As much as we may learn about God, there is always something more, there is always a deeper depth, a brighter light. And our faith isn't just about us!

What would you like to find as you go through life. I have known millionaires who felt that their wealth, though wealth had been a goal earlier on, was not everything. Most people eventually discover that they just wanted to find happiness. Wealth without happiness seems to lose its meaning. But… how do you seek happiness?

Happiness is not found in, or, as an abstract idea. It usually comes with relationships; especially with a relationship to God. So we need to seek out relationships that enrich our happiness. Even moreso, we need to be the reason someone else is happy. So… we seek the happiness of others. I like to see our purpose as that of bringing people to a more fulfilling relationship with God. Paul said he had learned "the secret of being well fed and of going hungry, of having plenty and of being in need" (Philippians 4:12). Paul had gained a "contentment" over the years. "There is great gain in godliness combined with contentment" (1 Timothy 6:6).

Rabbi Hyman Schachtel (1954) proposed that "**happiness is not having what you want, but wanting what you have.**" Next chapter, I will be talking about "treasures on earth" and "treasures in heaven", respective to what to keep and what to throw away. Knowing what we *want* is oftened determined by the lens through which we see things. And we need to see things through the lens of eternity, heaven, happiness.

I'm always sad to hear about some famous couple that had great wealth but who were no longer "happy" together. They "had it all," but they discovered what I said already, that without happiness the wealth loses its meaning. This life is a time to seek. Search for happiness! When we search together, the joy of searching multiplies!

A Time to Lose

What do you have that you can't lose? We humans are frail in so many ways. We can lose everything, even our health. But we can never lose the love God has for us. Yes, we can make God sad, we can disappoint God. We can reject God, fall away, go astray and sin; but God still loves us. That's what we all need to seek! With the lens of faith, we can see this truth, we can rediscover the hope of the treasures we have in heaven.

We might think we have a reputation that can't be lost. Our good character, our history, our good example. "A good name is to be more desired than great wealth, and favor is better than silver and gold" (Proverbs 22:1). But what are character and example when we go astray. Think of the Prodigal Son. He lost it all, but the one thing he felt he could still rely on was his father. And his father was gracious! Likewise, our Father, God, is gracious; and wants us to seek Him. The good news is that "everyone who searches finds" (Matthew 7:8).

What we need to lose is the pride we have in our status, or, our degree of attainment. We may have advanced so far that we think we are better than most people. Wealth and accomplishments don't make us better than others. Some of the millionaires I have known are still greedy, they still want more. They can be real fools to the rest of "us." Lose the attitude! The millionaires I have appreciated in my life's journey are the ones who saw beyond themselves and gave generously to God's purposes. Like the stones to be thrown away, we all need to cast off the stumbling blocks of selfishness and see ourselves as God sees us. Like Job, "Naked I came from my mother's womb, and naked shall I return there; the Lord gave, and the Lord has taken away; blessed be the name of the Lord" (Job 1:21).

SCRIPTURES

To discover more about what the Bible says about seeking and losing, here are some scripture passages that will help to inspire us:

Jeremiah 29:13 – When you search for me, you will find me; if you seek me with all your heart.

Psalm 63:1 – O God, you are my God, my soul thirsts for you; my flesh faints for you, as in a dry and weary land where there is no water.

Psalm 139:1-3 – O Lord, you have searched me and known me. You know when I sit down and when I rise up; you discern my thoughts from far away. You search out my path and my lying down, and are acquainted with all my ways.

Isaiah 55:6 – Seek the Lord while he may be found, call upon him while he is near.

Matthew 6:33 – Strive first for the kingdom of God and his righteousness, and all these things will be given to you as well.

Matthew 10:39 – "Those who find their life will lose it, and those who lose their life for my sake will find it."

Philippians 3:7-8 – Yet whatever gains I had, these I have come to regard as loss because of Christ. More than that, I regard everything as loss because of the surpassing value of knowing Christ Jesus my Lord…

Hebrews 11:6 – Without faith it is impossible to please God, for whoever would approach him must believe that he exists and that he rewards those who seek him.

2 Kings:7:15 – So they went after them as far as the Jordan; and the whole way was littered with garments and equipment that the Aramaeans had thrown away in their haste.

Matthew 16:25 – "For those who want to save their life will lose it, and those who lose their life for my sake will find it."

Philippians 4:11-12 – Not that I am referring to being in need; for I have learned to be content with whatever I have. I know what it is to have little, and I know what it is to have plenty. In any and all circumstances I have learned the secret of being well fed and of going hungry, of having plenty and of being in need.

WHAT TO DO

Be content with what you have!

Realize that everything you have is a gift from God.

Think: What would you still have if you lost "everything"? What are some of the "things" you take for granted?

See your treasures from God's point of view. What do you really have?

Ask yourself, how does God give "rewards to those who seek him" (Hebrews 11:6)? What are those rewards?

Look at what you "have" through the "lens" of happiness. How do some things seem different when you do?

A PRAYER

Almighty God, You have called us to seek out Your Kingdom and Your righteousness, and You have promised that everything else will fall into place when we do. Guide us in such a way that we will search for You with our whole hearts. And help us seek for the things You want us to find. Let happiness become our purpose with You, for the sake of others, and for Christ's sake. This I pray in Jesus's name. Amen.

A POEM

Be the Real You

Before you lost your reputation
        You used to be so sweet.
But you wanted to be known as someone fun.
        Goodness just seemed obsolete.
In my mind, though, you're still pure;
        You're even still a little shy.
You have a smile that will endure.
        Your eyes are like the sky.
Let's go watch the sun go down
        And see the stars come out.
Let's listen to the simple sound
        The shoreline's all about.
              I'll treat you like the girl I knew,
              And let you be the real you.

CHAPTER 10

A TIME TO KEEP, AND A TIME TO THROW AWAY

Do not store up for yourselves treasures on earth,
where moth and rust consume and where thieves break in and steal;
but store up for yourselves treasures in heaven,
where neither moth nor rust consumes
and where thieves do not break in and steal.
For where your treasure is, there will your heart be also.
Matthew 6:19-21

This dichotomy could fit in well with the dichotomies of Chapter 4 and Chapter 7 – "a time to break down and a time to build up;" and, "a time to throw away stones, and a time to gather stones together." Certain stones have already been an issue respective to what to "throw away." But, now we will find even more to throw away. "Cast all your anxiety on him because he cares for you" (1 Peter 5:7). We need to "throw away" our anxieties to God.

The issue in this chapter is less about objects to throw away, though it still can be, than it is about our posture toward "things." Our "treasures" are at issue. We are supposed to understand eternal, heavenly treasures as the things we need to keep, and the things of the world as the stuff to cast away, or, at least, not store up or accumulate. Remember how Paul said that "friendship with the world is enmity with God" (James 4:4). Where is your heart?

A Time to Keep

Some people are collectors. They never throw anything away. It's not sinful, necessarily, but some "stuff" *can* be a hindrance, like the stones and stumbling blocks we need to throw away. There is a lucrative business in storage these days. We've just got too much "stuff."

Many of us keep sad memories way too long. Many hold grudges. Letting go and looking forward is better. It is hard to go forward when you are too tied to the past. Of course some of our connections to the past are very sweet. And we need them.

But there is a time for keeping. We need to keep those things that truly enrich our lives; the things that have meaning. I have pictures from my children when they were little that I have saved for decades. Now, it is a special treat to bring them out to show them to them. It brings back so much love, and it touches our hearts when we see them together.

Keep the commandments. Keep your vows, your promises, your word. Keep watch… over your heart, over your soul, over your family. Keep on guard against evil. Keep the peace.

Financially speaking, keeping can be a matter of having a life savings. There are a lot of practical issues with this in mind, but ultimately, we are stewards of the resources in our lives. We are not supposed to seek wealth, necessarily, but God's purposes for us, and for our money. Hold on to what is good, keep a positive attitude. Keep on trying. Keep doing good.

There is a time to keep!

A Time to Throw Away

Have you ever downscaled? The idea there is the removing of clutter. Having moved several times to serve a new congregation in a new community, I have always been amazed at how much "stuff" we had acquired/accumulated. Every time, we gave a lot of stuff away. Still, I feel like I have a few more tons of "stuff" than I ought to have… especially books. Downscaling can be a healthy exercise. What we decide to keep says a lot about us.

It's been hard to let go of some of the things that were gifts over the years. But, sometimes there comes a time to throw stuff away.

It can be very relevant to throw some things away. Listen to this hard lesson from Christ: "If your right eye causes you to sin, tear it out and throw it away; it is better for you to lose one of your members than for your whole body to be thrown into hell. And if your right hand causes you to sin, cut it off and throw it away; it is better for you to lose one of your members than for your whole body to go into hell" (Matthew 5:29). I don't believe we need to throw away eyes and hands, but…we need to realize that anything is better than hell. The negatives in our minds need to be tossed. The lies, the twisted ideas about liberals or conservatives, politics, the ego fueled visions of grandeur… all need to be tossed. A mature faith and a reasonable mind usually sort out most of this. But. There needs to be a time to throw them away.

Letting go of the past in order to go forward can always be relevant.

There is a time to throw away!

SCRIPTURES

To discover more about what the Bible says about keeping and throwing away, here are some scripture passages that will help to inspire us:

> 1 Timothy 6:6-8 – Of course, there is great gain in godliness combined with contentment; for we brought nothing into the world, so that we can take nothing out of it; but if we have food and clothing, we can be content with these.

> Psalm 49:17 – For when they die they will carry nothing away; their wealth will not go down after them.

> Psalm 23:6 – Surely goodness and mercy shall follow me all the days of my life, and I shall dwell in the house of the Lord my whole life long.

> Matthew 5:13 – You are the salt of the earth; but if the salt has lost its taste, how can its saltness be restored? It is no longer good for anything, but is thrown out and trampled under foot.

Matthew 24:42 – "Keep awake therefore, for you do not know on what day your Lord is coming."

Luke 6:38 – "Give and it will be given to you. A good measure, pressed down, shaken together, running over, will be put into your lap; for the measure you give will be the measure you get back."

Luke 12:15 – "Take care! Be on your guard against all kinds of greed; for one's life does not consist in the abundance of possessions."

John 14:15 – "If you love me, you will keep my commandments."

1 John 4:18 – There is no fear in love, but perfect love casts out fear.

1 John 5:21 – Little children, keep yourselves from idols.

Isaiah 26:3 (KJV) – Thou wilt keep him in perfect peace, whose mind is stayed on thee: because he trusteth in thee.

WHAT TO DO

Downscale. Do you have things you never use, tools, cookware, bric a brak? Can you let go of some things?

Keep a positive attitude. Let go of negativity. Does that sound too new-age?

Keep the commandments, the law, a healthy set of morals.

Give away the clothes you don't/can't wear any more. My wife died in May. In July, I had a friend go through all her clothes. She kept some things, the rest went into bags for a free clothing distribution "closet".

Think of the "treasures" in your life. Do you have treasure in heaven? What are those treasures?

"Keep awake! For you do not know on what day your Lord is coming."

A PRAYER

Almighty God, you call us to lay up treasures in heaven. Help us to understand what that might mean in our lives. Give us grace to be wise with our resources on earth, and help us know what to hold on to and what to let go. Especially give us the wisdom to let the past be the past so we might seek a future filled with your blessings. This I pray in Jesus's name. Amen.

A POEM

Trust the Future

I trust the future that is promised by my Lord.
I trust His perfect comfort; His righteousness restored.
I trust the love and mercy, forgiveness, and the grace
That has been witnessed, now, throughout the human race.

I will keep a watch over the truth that I believe.
I will hold fast to the blessings of all that I receive.
My cup, it has been lifted; my cup now overflows.
I'm touched to see the wonders of all that Jesus shows.

Cast off the doubt and darkness, the sickness that is sin,
And welcome then the opened heart where joy can enter in.
Accept the Spirit's power working to renew
The image of God's glory that is still inside of you.

Prepare for us Your glory, Lord. Prepare for us a place
Where we can know Your presence, and see You face to face.

CHAPTER 11

A TIME TO TEAR, AND A TIME TO SEW

> Yet even now, says the Lord,
> return to me with all your heart,
> with fasting, with weeping, and with mourning;
> rend your hearts and not your clothing.
> Return to the Lord your God,
> for he is gracious and merciful,
> slow to anger and abounding in steadfast love,
> and repents from punishing.
> Who knows whether he will not turn and relent,
> and leave a blessing behind him…
> Joel 2:12-14

Rending your garments was a sign of grief. Job did it (1:20). It was an extreme expression of pain when the High Priest did it after hearing Jesus admit He was the Son of God and saying, "'But I tell you, 'From now on you will see the Son of Man seated at the right hand of Power and coming on the clouds of heaven.' Then the high priest tore his clothes and said, 'He has blasphemed! Why do we still need witnesses?'" (Matthew 26:64-65)

Tearing, or, rending; and sewing, or, mending are perfect symbols of destroying and restoring. Tearing is an image used respective of the kingdom of Israel. When "Ahijah laid hold of the new garment he was wearing and tore it into twelve pieces. He then said to Jeroboam: Take for yourself ten pieces; for thus saith the Lord, the God of Israel, 'See, I am about to tear the kingdom from the hand of Solomon, and will give you ten tribes…'" (1 Kings 11:30-31).

But Joel called the faithful to rend their hearts and not their clothing (2:12). The idea of rending, or, tearing their clothes was that it was symbolic of tearing their hearts. It was an act, in Joel, of repentance, returning to God, so that God would "relent" from punishing the nation for their sins.

A Time to Tear

Nowadays, we often speak of broken hearts, not torn hearts. The idea is just as tragic. It's hard to imagine that there would ever be a proper time for breaking someone's heart. But I can testify to many broken heart experiences. In the United Methodist Church, it seems to be a built in reality. We often know that a Pastor will one day leave. Pastors know it too. It can come very unexpectedly, and, it can come very deliberately. The Bishop and the Cabinet, together, discern where a congregation may need a new Pastor. When it was felt that I should be removed from a congregation I cared for in order to serve a different congregation (for which I would also care), it was like they were breaking us up, and it broke my heart, and many hearts in the congregations I served.

That's just one example of a time to tear. There can be many other examples. I imagine politicians might experience such times. People in business might be sent to a new branch in another state. Colleagues, neighbors, and friends, will feel heartbreak due to the drastic change. The loss of a loved one can be heartbreaking. Of course, couples who get divorced, may also realize that it is a time to tear. Sometimes, it can be a life-saving event for one or both partners in the relationship. The mending, however, may come with the new relationships that can be created. In each experience, the tearing apart can be an opportunity for a second, or third, or… chance in life. Eventually, there is mending that can happen. So there is usually a time to sew.

A Time to Sew

The fabric of our lives can sometimes unravel. When my bluejeans became threadbare, and holes appeared, I usually sewed patches on them. That was the cool thing to do way back then. Nowadays, it is holey jeans that are cool. No patches, just holes. I usually used pieces from another pair of pants that were not so threadbare. Many times, I used the fabric from an old guitar strap. And, if I do say so myself, it looked kind of cool. But, when I did that, I eventually learned what Jesus said about using some new fabric to patch some old fabric. "No one sews a piece of unshrunk cloth on an old cloak; otherwise, the patch pulls away from it, the new from the old. And a worse tear is made" (Mark 2:21).

Jesus may be talking about the difficulty of mixing traditional and contemporary ways, but there is just another type of heartbreak. We may cherish the traditions of the past, but, we also need to learn the relevance of the new. It's like the man who always rode a bicycle being introduced to the automobile. He didn't like it at first because he couldn't figure out how to pedal it.

Today's churches sometimes have a struggle with blending contemporary songs with traditional worship. It often has to do with what musical instruments are being used. To those who were reluctant about some of the new songs, I would usually say, "Every song was new to you once!" "Doesn't the Bible tell us to sing to the Lord a new song?" (Psalm 98:1).

If you've ever seen the musical "Fiddler on the Roof" you see both the power of tradition, and, the need for new ways. The changes that occurred in the 20th Century were some times of great heartbreak, and, lots of mending. We still need mending in the modern world. And there will always be times of great heartbreak.

I particularly like the image of restoration that comes with this dichotomy. Tearing and sewing, or, rending and mending, can bring very positive hopes. The material from the wedding gown that is used in a daughter's Confirmation dress. The need to let-out or take-in the seams of our clothes to make them seem like new again. Even patches have a positive side. I like what Peter said: "And after you have suffered a little while, the God of all grace, who has called you to his eternal glory in Christ, will himself restore, support, strengthen, and establish you. To him be the power forever and ever. Amen" (1 Peter 5:10-11). There's the lens we need respective to our faith. No matter how broken or brokenhearted we may be, God will restore us. No matter how torn things may seem, there will be some sewing in the future.

One final image: The tearing of the Temple Curtain in the Holy of Holies (Matthew 27:51) is a symbolic image that tells us that God would no longer be veiled from the faitnhful. By the death of Christ, nothing would separate the believer from the presence of God. God makes all things new!

SCRIPTURES

To discover more about what the Bible says about tearing and sewing, (rending and mending), here are some scripture passages that will help to inspire us:

> Matthew 27:50-51 – Then Jesus cried again with a loud voice and breathed his last. At that moment the curtain of the temple was torn in two, from top to bottom
>
> Genesis 3:7 – Then the eyes of both were opened, and they knew that they were naked; and they sewed fig leaves together and made loincloths for themselves.
>
> Genesis 3:21 – And the Lord made garments of skins for the man and for his wife, and clothed them.
>
> Numbers 14:6 – And Joshua son of Nun and Caleb son of Jephuneh, who were among those who had spied out the land, tore their clothes.
>
> 1 Kings 21:27 – When Ahab heard these words, he tore his clothes and put sackcloth over his bare flesh; he fasted, lay in the sackcloth, and went about dejectedly.

Job 1:20 – Then Job arose, tore his robe, shaved his head, and fell on the ground and worshiped.

Isaiah 64:1 – O that you would tear open the heavens and come down, so that the mountains would quake at your presence…

Luke 5:36 – He also told them a parable: "No one tears a piece from a new garment and sews it on an old garment; otherwise the new will be torn, and the piece from the new will not match the old…"

1 Peter 5:10-11 – And after you have suffered a little while, the God of all grace, who has called you to his eternal glory in Christ, will himself restore, support, strengthen, and establish you. To him be the power forever and ever. Amen.

WHAT TO DO

Think about some of the ways you have experienced grief. How do you feel about rending your clothes?

Be a mender. When the fabric of life becomes threadbare, be a patch!

Rend your heart. What might that mean?

Consider some of the ways people can experience broken hearts. How have you had your heart broken?

Think about some of the traditions you may know. How are they still strong? How are some of them becoming obsolete?

Watch, or, rewatch the musical "Fiddler on the Roof." What does it do for you?

Look at a quilted bedspread or blanket. Who created it? Think about the labor that went into it's creation. And think about the different pieces of material that were used, the patterns, and the colors. What makes is special? For someone there were lots of times to sew!

A PRAYER

Almighty God, You have woven the fabric of our lives and given us the spiritual threads to put all the pieces together; guide us in the rending and mending of Your world. Inspire us to do our part in bringing about the restoration that makes all things new. And give us grace to mend by healing after we have felt torn apart by grief. This we ask in Jesus's name. Amen.

A POEM

It Just Will Take Time

They'll stitch you together, but the cuts will be deep.
I'll be beside you. There's a vigil I'll keep.
My heart will be breaking. My eyes won't be dry.
I know this is scary. It's all right to cry.
When you will awaken, you'll still feel numb.
But soon you will move again, and you *will* overcome.
You will be as good and as new as can be.
And in time you'll look back and be able to see
That this was just part of a much larger plan,
And you will be able to be all that you can.

For now we'll be praying that all will be well
As you go through this trial, this sample of hell.
And we will be glad when this dark time will end.
It just will take time for your body to mend.

CHAPTER 12

A TIME TO KEEP SILENCE, AND A TIME TO SPEAK

> Even fools who keep silent are considered wise;
> when they close their lips, they are deemed intelligent.
> Proverbs 17:28

The time to speak is when people need to learn the truth. The time to keep silent is when we need to listen. Listening is not easy when you've got something to say. It's nearly impossible when we have questions. But when we hope to learn, we need to listen. If we are always talking, we can't absorb what the teachers are saying. There are always opportunities to be quiet and discover the sounds of the world. I like to listen to music. I particularly like to listen to the lyrics of the songs I like. But, I need to take the time to listen. Listening takes time. We are giving someone else our time when we are listening to them. To listen is to give a gift!

Meanwhile, I am a preacher. I get to speak while others *have* to listen! Our words can be light in the darkness, they can guide those who are lost. And they can inspire some in their journeys. If you were asked for directions, it would be wrong to be silent, especially if you knew how to tell those asking what you knew about how to get where they want to go.

A Time to Keep Silence

We don't always have to be doing something! For example, when we're waiting, we can just be quiet. It is a good time to center ourselves. Silence helps us do that. "Be still and know…" (Psalm 46:10). As we wait, we can "collect" our thoughts. I like that concept, *collecting thoughts*. Sometimes, when we are silent, we can review our day, or, days. A good time to be silent, or at least, quiet is in a library. I am fairly quiet when I am reading. So are others. It's a good time to have less distractions.

I have known many people who, as soon as they get home, turn on the television or radio, or their music player (I almost said "record player"). Just because it's there doesn't mean it has to be "on" all the time. Being silent can be a way of "turning off" the "noise" of our lives. I like what the Proverb above says: "Even fools who keep silent are considered wise." Sometimes, it's just better to keep our mouths shut! Why open them and prove our ignorance? I wish more politicians would practice this idea!

Of course, when someone else is speaking, we need to listen. We should not interrupt. It is a kindness. Although many people might not be listening sincerely, because they are really just waiting for their chance to speak, it is still good to listen to others. It validates them, and, we might learn something from them.

But the best time to listen is when we can learn something. A teacher can actually be imparting truths we ought to know. That's definitely a time to keep silence.

A Time to Speak

When we speak, we need to speak "so that your words may give grace to those who hear" (Ephesians 4:29). The best time to speak is when others need to hear the truth. I like the joke about how the person who talks to themselves is just wanting to hear an expert opinion!

I said above that our words can be light in darkness. People need to hear the truth. Jesus said,

> "You are the light of the world. A city set on a hill cannot be hid. No one after lighting a lamp puts it under a bushel

basket, but on the lampstand, and it gives light to all in the house. In the same way, let your light shine before others, so that they may see your good works and give glory to your Father in heaven." (Matthew 5:14-16)

You are the light – The "you" is plural there. Sometimes we might not want it to mean "us". Individuals might want to say, "That doesn't include me!" They hesitate because they might think that "If I accept the idea that it does include *me*, then I'm responsible to be the light, or at least part of it." Be part of the light! Let your words bring light!

A city set on a hill cannot be hid – It is exposed for all to see. If all can see it, especially at night, its lights become a sign of the city's ability to be a place of refuge. If the city cannot be seen, it would just be passed by. No one would seek its shelter. I believe we need to be not just light, but like city lights at night!

No one after lighting a lamp puts it under a bushel basket – To hide a lamp might suffocate the flame. To hide the lamp would defeat its purpose. Now, if your faith is like a light, it should be a guide for yourself, and, for others.

But on the lampstand – The more we show the light, the more others will be able to see by it. Likewise, the more we share our faith, the more others will begin to believe!

Let your light shine before others – Not just a suggestion; a command. Consider the meaning behind Jesus' words when He said, "Whoever would save their life will lose it, and whoever loses their life for my sake will find it" (Matthew 16:25). The secret of perpetual light is feeding the flame, letting it spread, giving light to other lamps by passing it from wick to wick, losing it to others. The "your" here, again, is plural!

At a youth retreat back in 1983, everyone had a candle. We stood in a circle around a map of the world. Holding our lit candles before ourselves, we could gaze around the circle and see one another's faces. "You are the light of the world," was said. And then everyone was asked to put their lit candle in special holders on the map in the middle of the circle. The world was covered by our lights. Then back in the circle, even though we had all given up (lost) our lights, we could still see each other's faces. In fact, it seemed even bighter than before. Putting our lights together made the whole world a brighter place. Let your (plural) light (singular) shine!

<u>That they might see your good works</u> – It's hard to do most good works with a lamp in one hand. That's why we put the light on a lampstand. Not only does it then give the light you need for yourself, but for "<u>all in the house</u>." Letting our light shine can be done by what we say, and, our actions can also speak as loudly as our words. The light of faith is fueled by good works. Always remember though, we are saved faith, not by our works.

<u>And give glory to your Father in heaven</u> – The purpose of it all, of spreading the light, is to glorify God. We don't just keep it to ourselves.

May all the words we speak bring light into the lives of others. Now is the time to speak! Doing so can glorify God!

SCRIPTURES

To discover more about what the Bible says about speaking and silence, here are some scripture passages that will help to inspire us:

<u>Silence</u>
Job 2:13 – They sat with him on the ground seven days and seven nights, and no one spoke a word to him, for they saw that his suffering was very great.

Psalm 141:3 – Set a guard over my mouth, O Lord; keep watch over the door of my lips.

Proverbs 10:19 – When words are many, transgression is not lacking, but the prudent are restrained in speech.

Proverbs 19:20-21 – Listen to advice and accept instruction, that you may gain wisdom for the future. The human mind may devise many plans, but it is the purpose of the Lord that will be established.

Ecclesiastes 9:17 – The quiet words of the wise are more to be heeded than the shouting of a ruler among fools.

Isaiah 53:7 – He was oppressed, and he was afflicted, yet he did not open his mouth.

Mark 3:4-5 – Then he said to them, "Is it lawful to do good or to do harm on the sabbath, to save life or to kill?" But they were silent. He looked around at them with anger; he was grieved at their hardness of heart…

Mark 15:5 – But Jesus made no further reply, so Pilate was amazed.

Luke 20:26 – And they were not able in the presence of the people to trap him by what he said; and being amazed by his answer, they became silent.

Revelation 8:1 – When the Lamb opened the seventh seal, there was silence in heaven for about half an hour.

Ephesians 4:29 – Let no evil talk come out of your mouths, but only what is useful for building up, as there is need, so that your words may give grace to those who hear.

<u>Speak</u>
Esther 4:14 – For if you keep silence at such a time as this, relief and deliverance will rise for the Jews from another quarter…

Proverbs 31:8 – Speak out for those who cannot speak, for the rights of all the destitute.

Isaiah 62:1 – For Zion's sake I will not keep silent, and for Jerusalem's sake I will not rest, until her vindication shines like the dawn, and her salvation like a burning torch.

Ezekiel 3:18-19 – If I say to the wicked, "You shall surely die," and you give no warning, or speak to warn them from their wicked way, in order to save their life, those wicked persons shall die for their iniquity; but their blood I will require at your hand. But if you warn the wicked, and they do not turn from their wickedness, or from their wicked way, they shall die in their iniquity, but you will have saved your life.

Matthew 18:15 – If another member of the church sins against you, go and point out the fault when the two of you are alone. If the member listens to you, you have gained that one…

Acts 18:9-10 – One night the Lord said to Paul in a vision, "Do not be afraid, but speak and do not be silent; for I am with you, and no one will lay a hand on you to harm you, for there are many in this city who are my people.

Romans 1:16 – For I am not ashamed of the gospel; it is the power of God for salvation to everyone who has faith…

Ephesians 4:15 – But speaking the truth in love, we must grow up in every way into him who is the head, into Christ.

Colossians 3:16 – Let the word of Christ dwell in you richly, teach and admonish one another in all wisdom; with gratitude in your hearts sing psalms, hymns, and spiritual songs to God.

2 Timothy 3:16 – All scripture is inspired by God and is useful for teaching, for reproof, for correction. And for training in righteousness…

Wait

Psalm 27:14 – Wait for the Lord; be strong, and let your heart take courage; wait for the Lord.

Psalm 62:5 – For God alone my soul waits in silence, for my hope is in him.

WHAT TO DO

Wait in silence! God will manifest to you what you need to know.

Listen…especially when you want or need to learn.

When you know the directions, tell them.

When it is quiet, collect your thoughts. What does that mean for you?

Turn off the noise in your life, at least, sometimes.

Try to be a good listener.

Spread the light! How is speaking a way to do so?

Ask yourself, Why was there silence in heaven at the opening of the seventh seal? (Revelation 8:1).

Speak out for those who cannot speak, for the rights of all the destitute (Proverbs 31:8).

A PRAYER

Almighty God, You created the universe with a word, and You continue to create blessings in our lives by Your word in scripture. So we need to listen in order to hear what You are trying to say to us. And then once we know what You have said, we need to repeat it so that others may hear. Give us grace to speak when others need to learn Your ways. And give us a sense of urgency for their sake, for they might never be willing to listen again. This I pray in Jesus's name. Amen.

A SONG

I Never Let a Day Go By

I never let a day go by
    Without telling you I loved you.
        Usually it was the first thing
            On my mind and in my heart.
Even now I want to say it
    I just like to hear the words
        It helps me to remember
            How my inspiration starts

I am so silent nowadays.
    It's quiet and you're gone.
        There's lots of great reminders though
            That tell me I was blessed.
The blessings don't just disappear
    They seem to echo every day.
        They're in the way I always feel
            Like I have just been kissed.

        It just feels good for me to say,
      "I love you" to you every day

CHAPTER 13

A TIME TO LOVE, AND A TIME TO HATE

> "You have heard that it was said,
> 'You shall love your neighbor and hate your enemy.'
> But I say to you, Love your enemies
> and pray for those who persecute you,
> so that you may be children of your Father in heaven;
> for he makes the sun rise on the evil and on the good,
> and sends rain on the righteous and on the unrighteous.
> For if you love those who love you, what reward do you have?
> Do not even the tax collectors do the same?
> And if you greet only your brothers and sisters,
> what more are you doing than others?
> Do not even the Gentiles do the same?
> Be perfect, therefore, as your heavenly Father is perfect."
> Matthew 5:43-48

"Let love be genuine; hate what is evil" (Romans 12:9).

"You shall love the Lord your God with all your heart, and with all your soul, and with all your might" (Deuteronomy 6:5).

It is never right to hate another person. They are created in the likeness of God. What we should hate is what they might do, their sin, the evil in their lives. We should hate the evil in this fallen world. We are supposed to love... even our enemies! (Matthew 5:44). There is a song that reminds us to love: "They will know we are Christians by our love." But Christians can also be known for the things we hate. And we hate evil. God hates evildoers (Psalm 5:5). God loves righteousness and hates wickedness (Psalm 45:7). So... there *can be* a time for hate.

But it is always time to love. Love is listed as the first fruit of the Spirit (Galatians 5:22). I've said it many times in my career, "We love others, not because of who they are, but because of who *we* are, and ...who God is." Love is even greater than faith and hope! (1 Corinthians 13:13). And we are supposed to Love God with all our heart, and soul and strength (Deureronomy 6:5). Luke adds "mind" when he reiterates this verse in Luke 10:27 before Jesus tells the story of The Good Samaritan (30-37). The words from Deuteronomy 6:5 are to be kept in our hearts. (v.6) "Recite them to your children and talk about them when you are at home and when you are away, when you lie down and when you rise. Bind them as a sign on your hand, fix them as an emblem on your forehead, and write them on the doorposts of your house and on your gates" (vs7-9). We are to think about our love for God <u>all the time</u>!

<u>A Time to Love</u>

We should always be loving.

How do we love? Well, how has God shown His love? First, God made us, gave us life, sustains us, and cares for us. So, we can love others by nurturing their lives, by enriching them in kind ways, and by caring for them with compassion. Second, God forgives us, redeems us from our sinfulness, and makes us righteous. So, we can do the same by not holding someone's sins against them, and by encouraging them in righteousness by sharing the grace of God. Remember, "love bears all things" (1 Corinthians 13:7). Finally, God has given us His kingdom, eternal life in Christ. So we can celebrate this in our midst; we can share the message, spread the light, and nurture the seeds of the Word.

Obviously, saying, "I love you," goes a long way. People like to hear it, and, people *need* to hear it. There is a shortage of love in the world today. Since "love is kind" (1 Corinthians 13:4b), often simple acts of kindness speak loudly enough for others to see our love. Since "love is patient"

(1 Corinthians 4a), we should be gentle with those who are struggling. Love can take so many forms, and in so many ways we can express our Christian love that people will know we are Christians. The best way to love someone, is, as Jesus did, give our lives for them. Now that doesn't always mean that we must die for them, but that we give ourselves in service to them, sacrificially. And we can do so because we have the Spirit of Christ working and dwelling in us. We need to "abide in love" (1 John 4:16).

It is always a time to love!

A Time to Hate

As long as there is evil in the world, we have something to hate. But, we hate it because we love God so much, and God hates evil.

God hates deceit and falsehood. God hates pride and rebellion against His purposes. God hates violence, war, and oppression, and, the abuse of His children. God hates idolatry and insincere worship. God hates arrogance and indifference. God hates selfishness and the neglect of others. God hates corruption and immorality. God hates grudges, resentment, and unforgiveness. The list could probably go on for a while, but I want to believe everyone will get my point. God is holy, and anything that is unholy is contrary to His desire for us. God made us to be holy. Heaven is a holy place, and in order to get there, we, who are sinful, have to be made holy. Jesus Christ makes us holy, but we must believe in His atoning sacrifice for our sin, His forgiveness, and, above all, His love for us. I don't always like such short summations of the work of God's grace, but, again, I believe everyone will get my point.

And the point is that there is a time to hate.

SCRIPTURES

To discover more about what the Bible says about loving and hating, here are some scripture passages that will help to inspire us (I am surptized that there are so many scripture passages that mention hate. Here is just a portion):

Hate

Psalm 5:5 – You hate all evildoers.

Psalm 45:7 – You love righteousness and hate wickedness.

Psalm 97:10 – The Lord loves those who hate evil.

Proverbs 6:16 – There are six things that the Lord hates, seven that are an abomination to him: haughty eyes, a lying tongue, and hands that shed innocent blood, a heart that devises wicked plans, feet that hurry to run to evil, a lying witness who testifies falsely, and one who sows discord in a family.

Proverbs 8:13 – The fear of the Lord is hatred of evil.

Proverbs 10:12 – Hatred stirs up strife, but love covers all offenses.

Matthew 6:24 – "No one can serve two masters; for a slave will either hate the one and love the other, or be devoted to the one and despise the other. You cannot serve God and wealth."

Matthew 24:10 – "Then many will fall away, and they will betray one another and hate one another."

Luke 6:27-28 – "But I say to you that listen, Love your enemies, do good to those who hate you, bless those who curse you, pray for those who abuse you."

John 12:25 – "Those who love their life lose it, and those who hate their life in this world will keep it for eternal life."

John 15:23 – "Whoever hates me hates my Father also."

Romans 12:9 – Hate what is evil.

Romans 12:21 – Do not be overcome by evil, but overcome evil with good.

Ephesians 4:31 – Put away from you all bitterness and wrath and anger and wrangling and slander together with all malice, and be kind to one another, tenderhearted, forgiving one another, as God in Christ has forgiven you.

1 John 2:9-11 – Whoever says, "I am in the light," while hating a brother or sister, is still in the darkness. Whoever loves a brother or sister lives in the light, and in such a person there is no cause for stumbling. But whoever hates another believer is in the darkness, and does not know the way to go, because the darkness has brought on blindness.

Jude 23 – Save others by snatching them out of the fire; and have mercy on still others with fear, hating even the tunic defiled by their bodies.

<u>Love</u>
Deuteronomy 7:9 – Know therefore that the Lord your God is God, the faithful God who maintains covenant loyalty with those who love him and keep his commandments, to a thousand generations…

Proverbs 3:3-4 – Do not let loyalty and faithfulness forsake you; bind them around your neck, write them on the tablet of your heart. So you will find favor and good repute in the sight of God and of people.

Jeremiah 31:3 – I have loved you with an everlasting love; therefore I have continued my faithfulness to you.

Micah 6:8 – Love kindness…

Romans 8:35 – Who will separate us from the love of Christ?

1 Corinthians 13:4-8, 13 – Love is patient and kind; love is not envious or boastful or arrogant or rude. It does not insist on its own way; it is not irritable or resentful; it does not rejoice in wrongdoing, but rejoices in the truth. It bears all things, believes all things, hopes all things, endures all things. Love never ends. ... And now faith, hope, and love abide, these three, and the greatest of these is love.

1 Corinthians 16:14 – Let all that you do be done in love.

1 John 4:12 – No one has ever seen God; if we love one another, God lives in us, and his love is perfected in us.

1 John 4:16 – God is love, and those who love abide in God, and God abides in them.

1 John 4:19 – We love because he first loved us.

WHAT TO DO

Be loving... always! Encourage others to be loving as well.

Hate evil... always! Encourage others to hate evil also.

Be patient and kind!

Consider what it might mean to say, "We love others, not because of who they are, but because of who *we* are, and ...who God is."

Consider how love is greater than faith.

Hate the things listed above that God would hate.

Be nurturing, enriching, and compassionate.

Rejoice in the truth!

A PRAYER

Almighty God, You can make us loving even when it seems impossible. We know that all things are possible with You; so help us to be kind and gracious; help us to do the things that will show how You are loving. And give us grace to tell others we love them even if they are sometimes like enemies. This I pray in Jesus's name. Amen.

A POEM

I Will Stand in Defense

I will stand in defense of all that is right
And battle the evil that darkens the light.
I will put up a wall that keeps falsehood out,
And I'll build a great tower that protects us from doubt.
May all that I do and may all that I say
Be a witness to all of our God's perfect way.

And may I be a shield for those who are meek,
And for those who are vulnerable, reckless, and weak.
Let me be a guide to God's shelter and grace,
So that peace may be found in the love we embrace.
And may all that is false, and perverse, and unkind
Be purged from our hearts and from each human mind.

I will fight for redemption, for freedom from sin.
Let us all join the battle, and may righteousness win.

CHAPTER 14

A TIME FOR WAR, AND A TIME FOR PEACE

"Blessed are the peacemakers,
for they will be called children of God."
Matthew 5:9

All worldly war is wrong. It is a sign that diplomacy broke down. It is a sign that oppressing minds seek conquest for the sake of some egomaniacal drive. People who seek war are sinful. Self-defense, on the other hand, is legitimized by the way it is a reaction to the cruelty of war. When one country, state, or town wants to control another country, state, or town, it is almost always led by someone who wants to have control. The purpose of any self-defense conflict should be peace, in the long run, not control. We would defend ourselves, our families, our "way of life," in order to return to peace. And peace is not just an absence of war, or conflict, it is the presence of reconciliation, of safety, and of good. Wellness.

Spiritual warfare, however, is right and necessary for the faithful. Nothing would bring us peace more than the defeat of evil. And we need to "overcome evil with good" (Romans 12:21). We need to love our enemies, as I said in the previous chapter. We should hate only what is evil. So, we should hate war. We should hate conflict and confrontation. We should hate all enmity. Peacemakers would seek conciliation, compromise, resolution, and rectification… "If it is possible, so far as it depends on you, live peaceably with all" (Romans 12:18).

A Time for War

In his Letter to the Ephesians, Paul says, "Our struggle is not against enemies of blood and flesh, but against the rulers, against the authorities, against the cosmic powers of this present darkness, against the spiritual forces of evil in the heavenly places" (Ephesians 6:12) It's as though there is an almost unseen reality against which we need to fight. I say "almost unseen," because it is manifested in the corruptive ways a lust for power and control sometimes possesses human beings, and turns them into agents of the evil of war and enmity.

What we need to do, says Paul is

> "Take up the whole armor of God, so that you may be able to withstand on that evil day, and having done everything, to stand firm. Stand therefore, and fasten the belt of truth around your waist, and put on the breastplate of righteousness. As shoes for your feet put on whatever will make you ready to proclaim the gospel of peace. With all of these, take the shield of faith, with which you will be able to quench all the flaming arrows of the evil one. Take the helmet of salvation, and the sword of the Spirit, which is the word of God…and pray." (Ephesians 6:13-18a)

This is the war we need to fight. This is how there is a time for war. And when we are ready for this battle, there can be peace.

A Time for Peace

Even when spiritual battles seems raging all around us, there is a time for peace. Peace is not necessarily a sense of serenity that wells up from within, or cascades over us somehow, but a posture. I love John 16:33 – "I have said this to you, so that you may have peace. In the world you face persecution (*tribulation* in the KJV). But take courage; I have conquered the world." In the Gospel of John, Jesus has told His disciples that though they would be scattered, He would not be alone "because the Father is with me" (John 16:32). Our firm stance before the struggles of life in this spiritual warfare is to know that Christ has conquered. Christ has overcome. Being in Christ, we too will conquer!

God is indeed *with* us all. We know we can have peace simply by accepting this reality. Christ overcomes, conquers the world. His name, Emmanuel, means "God with us" (Isaiah 7:14; Matthew 1:23). This we need to trust, even while the spiritual battles are raging, and, even when the people of the world are embattled. My inner peace, however, doesn't really help those soldiers who are fighting against some worldly enemies, until I begin to do what I can to help others defend themselves somehow. To me that means that I need to be a partner in peacemaking, standing firm against the forces of evil. How? By advocating for justice in every regard, seeking goodness, love, a truce, and resolution. We, who believe, need to proclaim that there is a time for peace!

One of the most difficult battles of all is in the fight against ignorance. I believe most worldly wars, and the climate wars are fought because there is something that is ignored about "the enemy." If it is not ignored, some flaw in our perceived enemy is ignorantly magnified out of proportion and lies are told to convince "our side" that there is a reason for conflict. When, however, we try to love our "enemies" (Matthew 5:44), we will get to know them in a different light. And we may get the oppressors to understand their enemies in a new light. Start with peace, for with peace we can love. And in love, there are no enemies.

SCRIPTURES

To discover more about what the Bible says about war and peace, here are some scripture passages that will help to inspire us:

> Romans 12:18 – If it is possible, so far as it depends on you, live peaceably with all.
>
> <u>War</u>
> Exodus 14:14 – The Lord will fight for you, and you have only to keep still.

Psalm 27:3 – Though an army encamp against me, my heart shall not fear; though war rise up against me, yet I will be confident.

Psalm 35:1-7 – Contend, O Lord, with those who contend with me; fight against those who fight against me. Take hold of shield and buckler, and rise up to meet me! Draw the spear and javelin against my pursuers; say to my soul, "I am your salvation." Let them be put to shame and dishonor who seek after my life. Let them be turned back and confounded who devise evil against me. Let them be like chaff before the wind, with the angel of the Lord driving them on. Let their way be dark and slippery, with the angel of the Lord pursuing them.

Psalm 46:9 – He makes wars cease to the end of the earth; he breaks the bow, and shatters the spear; he burns the shields with fire.

Matthew 26:52 – Then Jesus said to him, "Put your sword back in its place; for all who take the sword will perish by the sword…"

2 Corinthians 10:3-4 – We do not wage war according to human standards; for the weapons of our warfare are not merely human, but they have divine power to destroy strongholds.

1 Timothy 6:12 – Fight the good fight of the faith…

<u>Peace</u>
Psalm 4:8 – I will both lie down and sleep in peace; for you alone, O Lord, make me lie down in safety.

Psalm 35:4 – Let them be put to shame and dishonor who seek after my life. Let them be turned back and confounded who devise evil against me.

Isaiah 2:4 – He shall judge between the nations, and shall arbitrate for many peoples; they shall beat their swords into plowshares, and their spears into pruning hooks; nation shall not lift up sword against nation, neither shall they learn war any more.

Isaiah 9:6 – …Prince of Peace…

John 14:27 – Peace I leave with you; my peace I give to you. I do not give to you as the world gives. Do not let your hearts be troubled, and do not let them be afraid.

Romans 8:6 – To set the mind on the flesh is death, but to set the mind on the Spirit is life and peace.

2 Corinthians 13:11 – Finally, brothers and sisters, farewell. Put things in order, listen to my appeal, agree with one another, live in peace; and the God of love and peace will be with you.

Philippians 4:6-7 – Do not worry about anything, but in everything by prayer and supplication with thanksgiving let your requests be made known to God. And the peace of God, which surpasses all understanding, will guard your hearts and your minds in Christ Jesus.

James 3:18 – A harvest of righteousness is sown in peace for those who make peace.

WHAT TO DO

Learn war no more!

Fight the good fight of faith.

Think about how God is fighting for you.

Don't be ignorant about the supposed "enemy."

Think about how you would act in self-defense.

Think: How much does it depend on you to live peaceably with all?

Be a peacemaker!

Put on the whole armor of God!

Think about what lies you have listened to about your supposed "enemies."

Consider some of the ways your heart may be "troubled."

Set your mind on the Spirit. It is "life and peace."

Worship! It's the best way to do battle!

A PRAYER

Almighty God, You have given us Your Spirit, and You have given us peace. You have called us to battle not against blood and flesh, but against the cosmic powers of this present darkness. Help us then to put on the whole armor of God and to stand firmly against evil. Help us proclaim the call to arms; and give us grace to help others in their spiritual battles as well. This we pray in Jesus's name. Amen.

A POEM

When I Struggle

When I struggle to find some peace,
There's a battle that just won't cease.
There's a challenge deep within
That I can't conquer, I can't win.

I can't follow any dreams.
I can't grasp the truth that seems
Elusive to my simple mind,
And so there is no peace that I can find
But I *can* surrender. I can pray,
And understand the faithful way
That discovers that You're always there
Whenever I'm immersed in prayer.
    And that's where peace is always found.
    And where You, my King, are always crowned.

CONCLUSION

NOW IS THE DAY OF SALVATION

> Besides this, you know what time it is,
> it is now the moment for you to wake from sleep.
> For salvation is nearer to us now than when we first became believers;
> The night is far gone, the day is near.
> Let us then lay aside the works of darkness
> and put on the armor of light;
> let us live honestly as in the day,
> not in reveling and drunkeness, not in debauchery and licentiousness,
> not in quarreling and jealousy.
> Instead, put on the Lord Jesus Christ,
> and make no provision for the flesh, to gratify its desires.
> Rom 13:11-14

No delays! The time has come! Is there a point of no return? What if there is? Then we'd better take advantage of the time we're given! "It is now the moment for you to wake from sleep!" (Romans 13:11). We need a spiritual eagerness respective of salvation. We need to want to experience it as if we were waiting in line for an amazing roller-coaster ride. This is not to say that faith is like a roller-coaster, though it can be sometimes. But… there should be an eagerness, a sense of the thrills to come. There is an immense joy and a powerful sense of immanence!

"Now is the acceptable time; see (behold), now is the day of salvation!" (2 Corinthians 6:2b) I like the word "behold." It seems more ominous. It seems more authoritative. It seems more biblical! It is like a triumphant loud *Tadaa*! People of faith need this sort of enthusiasm. After all, "there is a time for every matter under heaven" (Ecclesiastes 3:1)! Exclamation Point! *Tadaa*! God "has made everything suitable ("beautiful" in the NIV) for its time" (Ecclesiastes 3:11)!

Maybe we have a problem with…timing. Our timing may seem off. If you've ever played music with others, you need to work together timing-wise. If you've ever watched people try to dance, or clap to the music, it isn't hard to see who's timing is off. Sometimes I think we are out of sync with God's timing. And yet, there is still a time for every purpose.

Give God your time, and God will give you eternity!

Eternity may seem like it's only a future thing, but it can begin now! Salvation is a *now* thing. And Paul said, "For salvation is nearer to us *now* than when we first became believers" (Romans 13:11b). There is more to being saved than just being saved. There is something we're still waiting for. God isn't finished with us yet. Most of us have not yet reached "maturity…the measure of the full stature of Christ" (Ephesians 4:13).

Now is the day! All we really have is *now*! Salvation is the road we're on and the destination we seek. This road is our destination, and it leads us forward. And it's an awesome road!

It takes us through birth and death; through planting the seeds of the kingdom and harvesting souls; from killing for food, to healing from wounds; through breaking down to our humblest state, to building us up with encouraging words; through weeping with those who weep and laughing with those who rejoice; through mourning to dancing; from throwing away the stones as we clear the fields, to gathering them for the building materials we need; from embracing the truth, to refraining from holding on to the past; through seeking to losing; through keeping promises, to throwing away what is unneeded; from tearing to sewing; from listening in silence to speaking the gospel; from loving what is good to hating evil; and through war against sin, to peace with Christ and being peacemakers.

We shouldn't think we will be doing all these things all at once, all the time; though many of them will naturally overlap, and many will interrupt our plans. But God gives us these times, and God gives us the ability to do it all. We are to participate in God's purposes… faithfully, gladly, in a spirit of fulfillment, with eagerness and expectation. It's salvation time! Salvation time has come. And we are to "Work out your own salvation with fear and trembling; for it is God who is at work in you, enabling you both to will and to work for his good pleasure" (Philippians 2:12b-31).

Ah… It is about God's pleasure, not ours! It is God's time! Time belongs to God!

SCRIPTURES

To discover more about what the Bible says about salvation, here are some scripture passages that will help to inspire us:

> Psalm 102:13 – You will rise up and have compassion on Zion, for it is time to favor it; the appointed time has come.
>
> Psalm 130:5 – I wait for the Lord, my soul waits, and in his word I hope; my soul waits for the Lord more than those who watch for the morning.
>
> Isaiah 49:8 – Thus says the Lord: In a time of favor I have answered you, on a day of salvation I have helped you…
>
> Romans 10:9-10 – If you confess with your lips that Jesus is Lord and believe in your heart that God raised him from the dead, you will be saved. For one believes with the heart and so is justified, and one confesses with the mouth and so is saved.
>
> Ephesians 4:13 – …until all of us come to the unity of the faith and of the knowledge of the Son of God, to maturity, to the measure of the full stature of Christ.
>
> Philippians 2:12b-31 – Work out your own salvation with fear and trembling; for it is God who is at work in you, enabling you both to will and to work for his good pleasure.

Titus 2:11-14 – For the grace of God has appeared, bringing salvation to all, training us to renounce impiety and worldly passions, and in the present age to live lives that are self-controlled, upright and godly, while we wait for the blessed hope and the manifestation of the glory of our great God and Savior Jesus Christ. He it is who gave himself for us that he might redeem us from all iniquity and purify for himself a people of his own who are zealous for good deeds.

Hebrews 2:3 – How can we escape if we neglect so great a salvation?

WHAT TO DO

Be eager about your salvation. Love your salvation.

Work out your salvation!

Think: "For salvation is nearer to us now than when we first became believers" (Romans 13:11). How does it seem closer? Does it ever feel further away?

Lay aside the works of darknes.

Put on the armor of light.

Live honestly.

Think: How awesome is salvation to you?

A PRAYER

Almighty God, You have saved me from my sinful state and set me free to live for Your heavenly Kingdom. Help me to proclaim the wonders of Your grace, the goodness of Your Way, and the glory of Your Truth. May the light I know set me on fire so others may see the blessings they can know. This I pray in Jesus's name. Amen.

A SONG

In Every Picture

In every picture I might paint
    God's grace would be the atmosphere.
There would be joy, as if a saint
    Was passing by or standing near.
        There would be love. There would be peace.
        And happiness would see release.

There would be hope in all our eyes,
    As if we all felt something more;
As if the next thing was some prize;
    As if we'd just walked through some door.
        There would be love. There would be peace.
        And happiness would see release.

And You would be the subject seen
    In every foreground of each site.
The landscape would be so serene,
    As if some gloom gave way to light.
        There would be love. There would be peace.
        And happiness would see release.

All our dreams would be the same,
As if our great salvation came.

Amen for now.

www.ingramcontent.com/pod-product-compliance
Lightning Source LLC
LaVergne TN
LVHW041617070526
838199LV00052B/3181